D0908148

POEMS FROM MAINE

Take Heart

Selected by Maine Poet Laureate

Wesley McNair

Down East Books

Copyright © 2013 by Wesley McNair

Individual poems copyright by poet

Reprinted with permission

All rights reserved

ISBN 978-1-60893-222-1

Design by Lynda Chilton

Printed in the United States

Down East Books
www.nbnbooks.com
Distributed by
National Book Network
800-462-6420

Distributed to the trade by National Book Network

Library of Congress Cataloging-in-Publication Data available upon request

For Joshua Bodwell
and David Turner

Contents

1
Heart Faces

The Place Inside the Place

Changes **3** of Heart

The World and Back Again

Introduction

I f we had set out to create a program that was more threatening to the connection between poetry and its audience, we could hardly have done better than the system we have in America today. Poetry books are routinely printed in runs of less than a thousand copies, and only a few are given reviews or shelf space in bookstores. Partly in self-defense, poets band together in groups or aesthetic schools and offer bookstore readings attended by fellow poets and a few of the like-minded, or university readings attended mostly by students pressed into service. Meanwhile the general public, standing at the edges of such events, decides that today's poetry is probably not for them.

Yet people outside of literary circles continue to value poetry. They understand the poem's unique power to express in a few words the feelings that matter most to us. That is why they turn to poetry on milestone occasions like weddings and funerals and commencement exercises. It is my mission as Maine Poet Laureate to find new ways of bringing poetry to the people, reminding them in the process that it is not only for special occasions, but for every day of our lives.

So, with the help of the Maine Writers and Publishers Alliance, I have edited and introduced for the past two years a weekly column for Maine newspapers called *Take Heart: A Conversation in*

Poetry, making it my first initiative. Each week, *Take Heart* features a previously published poem by one of our state's poets, some from the past and most from the present. The column will last for the five years of my term as Poet Laureate. *Take Heart* now appears in thirty newspapers and newsletters across the state, with a combined circulation of well over 250,000 readers. When you put that figure together with the hundreds more who have access to the column through the Websites of dailies, the Maine State Library, the MWPA, and my Poet Laureate page on Facebook, the number of potential readers increases dramatically.

The responses to *Take Heart* have come from all quarters. I've received thanks by email from both the poets whose work has been reprinted and readers who have affected by it. Scores of the column's poems have been mailed and emailed in the enthusiasm of discovery. They've been displayed in grade schools and used for high school and prison classes in creative writing. A full set was copied to help a man fighting an extreme form of dementia learn once again how to read.

I am of course pleased by the popularity of the column, but no less pleased by the visibility it has given Maine's poets, proving both the relevance of figures long gone from the literary scene and the quality and diversity of our current writing. Who knew there were so many good poems being written in our state? How many other states could match such a production? When I started this initiative, I hoped to bring poetry to the people of Maine; now, I am proud week by week to bring them *this* poetry, and these poets, whose best work richly deserves a wide readership.

This anthology contains the first two years of poetry from the *Take Heart* initiative begun in May of 2011 — poems about wishes, pleasures, and sorrows; poems about familiar experiences you only thought you knew; poems that will inspire tears and laughter and help you to carry on. I offer them with thanks to Joshua Bodwell, Executive Director of MWPA and a partner in this laureateship; David Turner, my special MWPA assistant for the *Take Heart* column; Michael Steere, my editor at Down East; and the poets of Maine, whose unique and astonishing vision this book celebrates.

Wesley McNair
Mercer, Maine

Heart Faces

1

Mr. Fix-It

Stuart Kestenbaum

My father never made anything or
fixed anything, even though we had
the obligatory tools in the basement,

to my great grandfather the carpenter,
the once-used brushes and the mysterious
cans of paint and shellac. And he never
cooked anything either, never turned

the coffee pot down to perk,
never cracked an egg and only once
that I remember barbecued steaks,
the smoke rising to heaven like a burnt offering

from the charred remains. When he returned
home at night, the smell of gas and oil
still close to his clothes, he'd settle on the couch
finishing a *New York Times* crossword puzzle while

keeping track of the Yankees on TV, until he
fell asleep, only to rouse when I'd change the channel.
"I was watching that," he'd mumble, though asleep,
and I'd believe him, but now I think he wasn't there

but had been at his domestic work, the night shift,
dreaming the lives of his children,
building a house of words, writing
the perfect story whose ending we never get to.

Peaches

Kate Barnes

Jenny, because you are twenty-three
  (and my daughter),
you think you know everything;
and because I am fifty-three
                (and your mother),
I think *I* know everything.
A week ago you picked up two green little peaches,
only half-grown and still hard,
from under the loaded peach tree
and put them on the kitchen window sill;
and I thought
  (though I didn't say a word):
they're too small, they will just rot
but I won't move them, Jenny put them there.

Now the summer is over and you are gone,
the mornings are cool, squashes conquer the garden,
the tree swallows have flown away, crickets sing —
and the sweet juice of your peaches runs down my chin.

Spaghetti Western Days

Annie Farnsworth

for Jacob

My son, just turned five
has not learned the rules about wild versus tame.
Always busy, transplanting field violets
and dandelions into my garden to make it
"more beautiful," smuggling toads
and millipedes into the house to keep for pets.
I mourn those small lives whose tiny,
dessicated remains I must chip from the windowsills,
shake from shoeboxes, and I try to explain
why we must leave nature where it is.

But this is a boy who snitches
my scotch tape and writing paper
to roll his own "cigarettes," who knows
that the good guys wear white hats
but he wants a black one anyway. A boy
with holsters and spurs, no horse in sight.
Days like this, when both front and back doors
flap like wings, and the big pine out back
flies a banner of kite tail,
I see that my doorstep is no boundary

and that there are frontiers I haven't yet
got eyes to see. And if I know anything,
just one damn thing worth knowing
in this lifetime I've learned it only since
this whirlwind of a boy
blew into town.

Roses

Thomas Carper

During the night of fever, as she lay
Between an exhausted wakefulness and sleep,
I sat beside her fearfully, in dismay
When her slow breathing would become so deep
It seemed that she might slip beyond recall.
Then I would touch her; then she would revive;
Then, when her eyelids opened and a small
Smile would greet me, hope would come alive.
With morning, the ordeal was over. Gone
Was every trace of illness. A soft rain
Had swept across the countryside at dawn,
So even our garden was made fresh again.
Then Janet went among our roses where
She and the roses shone in luminous air.

Cullen: Four Days Old, Waking

Preston H. Hood

I hug my first grandson rock him back
& forth above the swaying white
daffodils,

hear his breath measured & calm,
& discover those sea-deep eyes that blink
from the water-music of sleep.

His tiny fingers open, close, embrace
my thumb, the moment sharing. Our lives
intertwine — branch toward light.

While he gazes up at me & into this world,
his eyelids flutter. I wonder what he sees, how he
thinks, what does he want to hear from me?

Four days, just four, too young
to focus or concentrate, yet somewhere
in sleep where he should be.

How irresistible in my arms: his head leaning
against my chest, the bright noon warming
around him. Peace composes his face.

His serene expression breathes love to me
in code. I hold him long enough against my cheek
to feel his pulse & yawning grin

awaken, & arouse in me a new beginning
where everything again is possible.
When I listen closely, I can almost hear him speak.

Eighty-Five

Elizabeth Tibbetts

"Shoo," she says and waves me away
like a big fly, though she's been happy to talk,
her lipsticked mouth taking me word by word
through her life: born in this town, never left,
widowed once, divorced twice, one daughter —
now dead — and forty years in the fish factory.

She and the girls loved every minute of it,
racing — piece work, you know. Gossip swooping
through the long room like a flock of starlings
while their hands, separate animals, filled
hundreds of tins day after day. Some days
they'd lift a big icy fish from the crate,

lay it on the boiler to steam, then eat it
with their fingers. There was never anything
so fresh. She fiddles with a button on her robe,
her nails roughly painted to match her mouth,
and no, she doesn't need help with her shampoo,
washing her creases, soaking her swollen feet.

She looks as though she never could get out
of that chair, but somehow it's easy
to see how she would have stood on a corner
in the South End, her feet in pumps, one hip
cocked, talking to a girlfriend, and seeming
not to notice the men from the shipyard loose
on Saturday night in their clean white shirts.

Watermelon

Susan Deborah King

There being not much of later
to enjoy it in, he suggested to me,
down-island neighbor, we cut it open
right now, the "personal-sized" melon
I brought, since he told me
I might as well take back home
the rhubarb pie I made for him in the hospital
because he preferred his fruit plain.
He could be plain in his speaking too!
Was it just the emotion of the moment
or was this the sweetest, juiciest, most rubiate
fruit a tooth ever sank into, bright
in the mouth as the July day outside
his shut in, TV-in-the-background house,
next to which sat his big red truck
with his late wife's name, same as his boat's,
emblazoned on the hood? Next to that
rose a yellow, cross-hatched
squared off mountain of idle,
due to his illness, traps. He was a strapping,
loose-jointed man, a hunter, a kidder, skipper
of any room he sauntered through.
When I got up to leave, he couldn't rise,

oxygen tubes pinched into his nostrils.
He took my hand — a surprise — looked
into my eyes and couldn't find the bottom.

In memory of Lyn Colby

1940

Sharon Bray

After they left the roller rink
and drove out of streetlight range,
he showed her Orion,
the one constellation
she still could name
into the year she died.

He could have seduced her
on the back seat blanket
of his downhill-fast Model A.

Instead he gave her one ripe orange,
which she took home to her mother.

Rained Out

Gerald George

After the Red Sox
blew their season
by losing three straight
in the playoffs to Chicago,
it rained for days.

"Coincidence," I said
over coffee down at
Archibald's One-Stop.

"Think what you like,"
Homer Jones replied,
buttoning up his slicker.
Then he walked out
and never spoke
to me again.

The Man Who Likes Cows

Sheila Gray Jordan

Thirty miles from the city,
past the first town
with a small name,
cows are in a field,
black and white Holsteins,
nudes with dairy nipples.

He stops the car,
opens the door on my side,
and I get out to see the cows
who look at us over their shoulders —
sloppy, dumb broads, wading
in milk and honeybees.

He is a man who likes cows.
But they are not to be coaxed,
cud-happy this spring day,
the grass green.
Something big — a bell or a sunset —
is necessary to move them.

Like Jove, "Speaking
their tongue. . . ," in his city suit,
he cups his hands: the Moo
rising from his groin,
a brazen klaxon,
helloing.

The call bends their thick skulls.
They lift their heads —
all eyes and ears —
coming on to crowd the fence.
I take his hand, make a fist of it
with its gold ring.

Love Is Not All: It Is Not Meat Nor Drink

Edna St. Vincent Millay

Love is not all: it is not meat nor drink

Nor slumber nor a roof against the rain,

Nor yet a floating spar to men that sink

And rise and sink and rise and sink again;

Love can not fill the thickened lung with breath,

Nor clean the blood, nor set the fractured bone;

Yet many a man is making friends with death

Even as I speak, for lack of love alone.

It well may be that in a difficult hour,

Pinned down by pain and moaning for release,

Or nagged by want past resolution's power,

I might be driven to sell your love for peace,

Or trade the memory of this night for food.

It may well be. I do not think I would.

Her Telling

Thomas R. Moore

When she told me
after she'd uncoiled the line
   with the steel stakes at the ends
   to set straight rows of peas
   clad in her denim cover-alls
   and tall rubber boots at seventy,
after she'd tossed garden stones
   onto the long windrow
   beyond the asparagus,
after she'd showed me
   the ants climbing the peony stalks
   to the hard buds and cupped hands
   beside the kitchen propane tanks,
and even after years of stirring
   green tomato mincemeat
   on the yellow Glenwood
   and tugging carrots
   from the hot August soil
   and snapping off ears of corn
   and letting me pick clean

the tree of seckel pears —
the hard tangy red fruit —
in October,
even forty years after that Christmas day
when she smashed the third floor door,
the children listening below,
to find her husband inside,
dead by his own hand,
my grandmother was stunned
by her own telling.

Mom Gets In One of My Poems

Martin Steingesser

"I thought I missed you, darling," she is saying on the phone.
"No, you woke me. It's 7:30."
"Oh —" she says, and then,
after a pause, "I didn't want to miss you."

How she won't be denied, how
I resist. Ninety-two, she's the kind
of goodness brings trouble, the powerful
voice calling me in

                evenings when I was a boy.
Maybe now it's her way
                to know she is okay.
Yesterday she called four times

for help with the date, days of the week
refusing to stay in their places.
"It's Saturday," she says, a questioning in her voice, adding,
"I'm so confused, it's embarrassing."

I can see her calendar: she's crossed off Friday
and forgotten, now maybe Saturday, too.
"I'm sorry, I cause so much trouble," she says, starting to cry.
"It's okay, Ma, I mix up days, too.

                                        Last week," I tell her,
"I drove to the wrong job."

                                        Suddenly she laughs,
and I know it's okay, for the moment
neither hearing the powerful voice.

Resurrection

Michael Macklin

The night Bobby Inch died
my father came home wild-eyed and crying.
A cattle truck charging through the dusk
caught the paper boy high on its horns,
threw him breathless to one side.

We wore the same shirt that day.
In flashing reds and blues,
my father saw the shirt, still
against the blacktop.
Felt me slipping from him.

Seeing Bobby's face,
some other father's son,
he raced home to rage and rant
and hold me, looking deep
into my wide open eyes.

Hands Reaching

Edward J. Reilly

A young boy, I was primed
for climbing, eyeing the oats bin
and its top, a crosshatching of boards
flaked with end-of-year fragments
left over from the top's
double duty as a hayloft.

I climbed and climbed, up the wooden
ladder, foot reaching gingerly for
the next step, hands gripping and
pulling, even a young boy's weight heavy.
I made it and exulted, exulted

all too soon. There came a time
when getting down was even more vital
than climbing up. But that distance
multiplied looking down, and neither hands
nor feet could move me down that crawl.

So I called, and my brother answered,
years older, years taller, strong
shoulders and long arms stretching,
reaching my straining hands, my hands
in his, the rest of me coming naturally.

Years later my brother, in his quiet, dark
living room reached and fell,
his large, much older body tumbling
to the floor, silent on a carpet brown as hay,
leaving me nights I dream about long
arms reaching for a frightened boy.

Sentences

Edward Nobles

The sledgehammer cracks
like my father's heavy shouts
until the stone starts to break.
The sound then is different.
Only a thumb's touch is needed.

The division is final.

Where He Went

Edward Nobles

My father gave up
wife children friends
dog car house every
worldly possession
traveling
far into a strange
space bottles
rotating shuffling clinking
searching vaguely for a genie
poof!

Housekeeping of a Kind

Patricia Smith Ranzoni

Once in a great while this house reeks
with remembrances of Wild Rose rage.
The payday cheap gallon kind.
The silent supper kind.
The don't pay any attention to your father
when he is drinking kind.
The fist on the kitchen table pounding kind.
The maybe if I listen he'll like me kind.
The sinks into Kem-tone cover-ups
and scats along once-a-year-painted
battleship gray, worn to the black,
linoleum floor kind.
The wraps around frozen pipes and spills up
through cracked ceilings
and out leaking roofs kind.
The thirty years later
has to be reminded it was renovated out kind.

Stubborn stain.

The Crossing

David Walker

At the far edge of the field, just in the shade,
my father waves; the heat cuts us in two
as I walk towards him. The stubble bleeds
yellow, then nearly white; it crunches like snow.

Into the sun I stride, erect in my cause
and body straining towards the other side.
Hands on his hips, my father watches me cross
calmly. I am revolved in the season's eye.

The sun leans in the distance, drawing a cloak
of pines slowly over its head; and still
he is waiting. Every year that I walk
his smile grows nearer. And I begin to smile.

If You Should Die Before I Do

Patricia Smith Ranzoni

I'll come wherever you're praised.
        Sit or stand in the back, *quietly*,

As I came whenever I came
        among those you've loved. As any

grateful heart knows not how
        to thank a source for song. At least

I knew you enough
        to comprehend *gave*. If you should die first,

I'll come bare-footed when you
        are alone. Don't worry, nothing tasteless

to clutter your grave,
        only my dust and petals and pollens

from my beds to sift into yours,
        and in this way I might come to hold you,

with the others,
        perhaps forever.

Old

Phillip Booth

Old, the old know cause to be bitter:

                                 they've seen

their children (as if they could tell)
insist they are growing deaf:

                         they've found

old friends invent new friends
to prove the old don't matter:

                          they have hardened

themselves to let memory rust out;
with only themselves to hold on to,

                         they have grown

beyond any surprise;
to get their way

                  they have aged again

to be children:
beyond control, they have gained

                         control

of every last life save their own.
They know it can get no better.

The Cross of Snow

Henry Wadsworth Longfellow

In the long, sleepless watches of the night,
   A gentle face — the face of one long dead —
   Looks at me from the wall, where round its head
   The night-lamp casts a halo of pure light.
Here in this room she died; and soul more white
   Never through martyrdom of fire was led
   To its repose; nor can in books be read
   The legend of a life more benedight.

There is a mountain in the distant West
   That, sun-defying, in its deep ravines
   Displays a cross of snow upon its side.
Such is the cross I wear upon my breast
   These eighteen years, through all the changing scenes
And seasons, changeless since the day she died.

The Power of It

Ted Bookey

Ruth woke sad today. Life, she says,
Has been behaving itself & hopeful
Expectations continue, so why now
Nameless dread & mope at sunrise?
What is it? What can it be?

I do not know but I will try.
To help her against it
— whatever it is
I put my arms around her,
Tell her, "What it is, is
There will come moments
When it is simply it."

I say this for myself
As much as for her —
That it is just it.

& it helps.

Sixty

Phillip Booth

Spring hills, dark contraries:

a glade in a fall valley,
its one flower steeped with sun.

The there and here of her.
The soft where.

The sweet closeness of when.

From dreams awake to turn to her.
Remembering, remembering.

And now again. Again.

Feasting

Elizabeth W. Garber

I am so amazed to find myself kissing you
with such abandon,
filling myself with our kisses
astounding hunger for edges of lips and tongue.
            Returning to feast again and again,
our bellies never overfilling from this banquet.
Returning in surprise,
in remembering,
in rediscovering,
such play of flavors of gliding lips
and forests of pressures and spaces.
The spaces between the branches
as delicious as finding the grove of lilies of the valley
blossoming just outside my door under the ancient oak.
"I've never held anyone this long," you said,
the second time you entered my kitchen.
I am the feast this kitchen was blessed to prepare
waiting for you to enter open mouthed in awe
in the mystery we've been given,
our holy feast.

Regeneration

Carolyn Locke

for Gerry

I heard how the starfish learns the world
through touch, how its chemical sense
leads it to the mussel bed, how it feels
its way around crevices sucking soft bodies
from their shells. You can't kill a starfish
in any usual way — chop one up
and it multiplies, filling the waters
with quintuples of spiny legs
reaching out from humped backs, and curling
around the deep purple shells on the rocky
bottom. Sometimes I think I know
what it is to know the world
through only the body. If I close my eyes,
I no longer feel where my body ends
and yours begins —
and I can believe your hands are mine
reaching for muscle,
a strange body becoming my own,
and in my ear an unfamiliar heartbeat
pumps new blood, breath no longer mine

doubles the lungs, my need
growing larger than what any body can hold
until there is only this way of knowing, this touch
that leads me, blind as the starfish,
to become what I cannot see.

The Place Inside the Place

The Glass Harmonica

Theodore Enslin

It snowed in far country
                    north and
beyond the trees.
As I went through the mirror
                    my breath froze
clouding it,
          and they saw me no longer
in the villages of spring.
                    I walked alone
across level plains,
          and my tracks disappeared
in the snow which went with me.
A wind rose
          playing on harpstrings
and reeds.
          There was nothing there, and my fingers
touched ice.
          A music
                    a music
                              an echo of music —
sound not a sound
          in the quiet north country —
the snow.

The Street

Lewis Turco

In the street the wind gutters, moving papers
and leaves into heaps or sworls.
The scraps of the year make some kind of pattern,
some calligramme of their own,
beyond the imprint of new snow.

Lightly, on the flourishes of silence,
on the heaps of leaf,
the snow touches and explores.
Finally, in folds of stillness,
flakes begin to form wrinkles of crystal.

By the time dusk deepens,
the wrinkles will be pure streams
drowning whatever is old.
Then, in the night, in the darkest hours,
the road will be a river of snow
aiming toward morning, lost at either end
in the curbs of vision.

Potatoes

Jay Davis

A family of potatoes lives under my sink.
They huddle there like wretched immigrants
in the hold of my kitchen, eyeing anyone
who peers down there with suspicion.
Despite the language barrier, they persist.
The more industrious put down roots.
They wear the same brown shabby coats
they brought from the old country,
though one or two are wrinkled now
from sleeping in them every night.
When the cupboard door is closed
I sense them in there, huddling closer,
muttering in their dark dialect, comforting
one another, whispering their dreams.

Winter Friends

Robert P. Tristram Coffin

The high cold moon rides through the frost,
The branches of the trees make lace
Along the drifted snow beneath,
There is no friendliness in the place,
Except in twelve small squares of light
Set in a house's midnight side.
Someone is awake with me
On the cold earth's wintry ride,
Through the pathways of the space,
He and I go on like friends,
Saying nothing, quietly,
To our separate unknown ends.

Essence

Stuart Kestenbaum

We hand-crank the drill through the maple's bark,
pound the metal tap into light inner layers

where the sap begins to flow, this life blood
that will make the leaves unfurl

in another two months, delicately
lined like the hands of a newborn.

But now we step over last year's leaves
and the year's before that

in patchy snow to gather what
we have taken from the tree, the gallons of sap

we boil down on our stove top,
moisture running off the kitchen windows

as we get down to its essence, over three gallons
to make a cup of syrup, so sweet

a transformation, I can't believe I could
have been a part of it. A world that doesn't

end in vinegar, ashes and regret,
but in a sweetness that rises every day

between earth and sky, traveling from the hole
in the side of the tree to our joyous mouths.

Porcupine

Tom Sexton

Its movement on
the ground is
that of a bag
of stones rolled
downhill, a spilled
quiver of black-
tipped arrows, but
now, on this
cold March morning,
it is raising the
dark flag of itself
to the top of
an ancient tree
like an explorer
claiming the world
in the name
of all that is Porcupine.

Mud Season

Alice Persons

After a brutal Maine winter
the world dissolves
in weak sunshine and water:
Mud sucks at your shoes.
It's impossible to keep the floors
or the dogs clean.
Peeling layers of clothes, you emerge
pale, root-like, a little dazed
by brighter light.
You haven't looked at your legs
in months
and discover an alarming new geography
of veins and flaws.
Last year you scoffed at people
who got spray-tanned
but it's starting to appeal.
Your only consolation is the company of others
who haven't been to Nevis
or Boca Raton,
a pale army
of fellow radishes,
round onions,
long-underground tubers.

Night Wind in Spring

Elizabeth Coatsworth

Two yellow dandelion shields do not make spring,
nor do the wild duck swimming by the shore,
so self-possessed, so white of side and breast,
nor, I suppose, the change in the land-birds' calls,
softened and sweetened to a courting note,
nor the new colors twigs are taking on,
not even the sun which rises early now
and lingers almost until dinner time.
We, too, are valid instruments; we, too, can say
if this be spring or only waning winter.
Tonight the wind is loud about our chimney.
There is no new moon in the sky, nothing but stars:
the Dipper upright on its shining handle,
Sirius bright above a neighbor's house,
and this wind roaming, not enough to scrape
a branch along the roof, or try the shutters
for one to bang. No, just enough to cry
and cry and cry against the stalwart chimney,
as though it were a wanderer who had come
down half the world to find one only door
and that door locked and nothing answering.

April and Then May

Kate Barnes

April and then May,
violets up in the field,
the ewes with their twin lambs;

time has decided
to turn into spring again
after all.

The maples are unfolding their leaves,
chives stand green at the kitchen door,
the black flies have decided to come back;

and the work mare has her new foal
capering over bluets in the pasture,
and the hall smells of daffodils;

and everything
is divinely ordinary —
the deep ruts in the field track,

the spring overflowing,
the excited swallows,
the apple trees

budding for perhaps the hundredth time —
and the pruned boughs budding too
that must bloom just where they lie.

Stealing Lilacs

Alice Persons

A guaranteed miracle,
it happens for two weeks each May,
this bounty of riches
where McMansion, trailer,
the humblest driveway
burst with color — pale lavender,
purple, darker plum —
and glorious scent.
This morning a battered station wagon
drew up on my street
and a very fat woman got out
and starting tearing branches
from my neighbor's tall old lilac —
grabbing, snapping stems, heaving
armloads of purple sprays
into her beater.
A tangle of kids' arms and legs
writhed in the car.
I almost opened the screen door
to say something,
but couldn't begrudge her theft,
or the impulse
to steal such beauty.

Just this once,
there is enough for everyone.

The Poet

Marta Rijn Finch

Heard you were moving in last week. Welcome.
You'll like it here. The people — most of them —
are friendly. You'll meet them tomorrow at church.
There's a bean supper afterward. Real nice folks.
Hard-working. But an old crone lives down
the street with a couple cats — three, maybe four.
Keeps to herself so we hardly know she's there.
She's got a daughter no one's ever seen;
visits her son somewhere over the border.
She has no flag, but hangs the hammock out;
that tells us she's in residence. We see it
from the shore — and smoke, of course, come winter.
They say she is a poet. I don't know.
I've never seen it. Can't be any good.
She read her poems once at the library,
but no one went. Not even the local teacher.
Just the librarian. She *had* to be there.
And a lot of folks drove up from away.

You don't write poetry, do you?

How to Catch a Poem

Robert Siegel

It begins with one leaf rubbing against another,
a light, a rift in a cloud, the weight of a feather
spiraling down, a ripple on the water —

its shape rising from the dark and fusing
with a sound, a touch, a peculiar scent. Now it begins
to show plumage, the gleam of a pelt, pausing

to stare with an ebony eye. One twitch — it's gone,
fled into that darker wood behind the eyes. Stunned,
you trace its tracks on paper, stumble,

pick yourself up and go down each sly
cheat of a path vanishing in a thicket, lie
still, listening for its breath, a twig breaking

where you think. . . . Avoid sleep, follow all day,
at night listen for its cry under the moon. Finally you may
gather enough to show its presence. Delay

finishing what you have. Take your time. Return home
and frame the cast of its footprint: that is the poem.

In Nightgowns

Sheila Gray Jordan

Nothing insists they get dressed.
Midmorning, like toddlers,
late parading in their pajamas,
they walk out of the house
in nightgowns.

What do they care who sees them
without a robe, appearing
in the first layer over
the Emperor's new clothes,
these elderly women

sweeping the steps, accommodating
an arthritic cocker spaniel,
dead-heading the lilies.
Or they proceed like butterflies,
pastel-bright, to flutter

from this to that, breezy —
not explaining —
in and out of sun and shade,
air reaching up under
a skirt.

Night

Louise Bogan

The cold remote islands
And the blue estuaries
Where what breathes, breathes
The restless wind of the inlets,
And what drinks, drinks
The incoming tide;

Where shell and weed
Wait upon the salt wash of the sea,
And the clear nights of stars
Swing their lights westward
To set behind the land;

Where the pulse clinging to the rocks
Renews itself forever;
Where, again on cloudless nights,
The water reflects
The firmament's partial setting;

— O remember
In your narrowing dark hours
That more things move
Than blood in the heart.

Some Clear Night

Gary Lawless

Some clear night like this,
when the stars are all out and shining,
our old dogs will come back to us,
out of the woods, and lead us
along the stone wall to the cove.
There will be foxes, and loons,
and a houseboat floating on the lake.
The trees will lean in, a lantern
swinging over the water, the creaking of oars.
Now we will learn the true names of the stars.
Now we will know what the trees are saying.
There is wood in the stove.
We left the front door open.
Does the farmhouse know
that we're never coming back?

Which World

Gary Lawless

There is a path
winding between Sitka spruce,
past totem poles stolen
from their island homes,
emptied of ashes and bones,
placed along the trail.
In the distance,
a volcano.
Raven flies
just above the surface of things, bald
eagle watching through
layers of air and water
for the fish
passing through,
shining in the cold
river like light
from another world,
everything moving, everything
moving to
come together, come together and

fall apart, again.
the water rushing.
the heart beating.
I am waiting for you
at the mouth of the river.

Driving Down East

Robert M. Chute

Crossing the Penobscot on Route One
we enter a different country. Our home state
on both sides of course, all part of the Main,
but the dull green rainbow bridge was a
suspension of disbelief as well as steel.

At Verona Island we expected a guard house
with a deadpan downeaster in oilskins to
silently check our visas and wave us through.

The houses were familiar clapboard and shingle
but smaller, pinched between wild lands,
barrens and ledges edging the sea. Life
on our inland lakes with its jumble of cobbles
seemed safe but not these wave-scoured ledges.

Life on the edge salts speech with words
as strange to us as to Summer People. Words
regional, individual, or invented to toll the tourists.

Everyone is "from away": we are, they are,   ✓
but all in one bag together in the final drag
dumped on the deck for culling.

The Red and Green Cement Truck

Richard Aldridge

rumbles by to where it's going, while
at an incline on the bed and
at right angles to the wheels
its mixer, shaped
like a big cocktail shaker, turns
upon an axis slowly, slowly,
blending the cement and water.

It is a feat as neat as
pat-your-head-and-rub-your-belly
but what I like still better is
to see in it
ourselves, we who do best
to use our heads for mulling, mixing
while with our feet
we keep on trucking.

The Dump Pickers

Bruce Guernsey

On Sundays
carting my trash to the dump
I'd see them swarming
the piles like gnats,
a whole family of pickers
straight from Mass:
Dad's suit, white
as the noon sky, Junior
in a polka-dot tie —
in bright, patent leathers
his small, pale sister.

From the highest of piles
Mother shouted orders
through a paper cup,
the men hurrying under
her red, high heels,
dragging metal to the pickup,
the little girl giggling,
spinning on her toes
through the blowing paper
like a dancer, a little twist
of wind in the dust.

Understory

Jim Glenn Thatcher

The old man had always been a mystery,
living out there on that abandoned logging road
in those miles of woods between the Parsonsfields.
Months would go by without anyone seeing him.
No one even noticed when he first went missing.
Gone for all of seven seasons before a hunter found him —
not in those open pine woods where they'd sometimes
seen him ranging, but tangled beneath the understory
less than a hundred yards behind his shack.
Stripped down to rags on a skeleton, bedded
in spears of burdock; ribs twined with creeper;
his skull filled now with the strangeness of other life,
the sun tracking its daily course of shadow and light
along the brow of the caves where his eyes had been.

When they went in to clean out his shack,
not expecting much — a rotting cot,
a very old sleeping bag, some utensils, one cup.
It was the notebooks that surprised them.
Piles upon piles of old notebooks, all of them full —
"Crawling with words," someone said. A library of wildness —
journal entries that seem written by the forest itself,

the woods he lived in become the woods living in him.
Passages of a feral intelligence hedging off into its hinterlands —
stories of stones, autobiographies of oaks and maples,
a runic hand-scrawl scratching itself into granite,
sand, leaf, bough, fin, fur, feather, claw,
the commonality of bark and blood and bone —
histories of a self gone Other. . .

Mantis

Robert Siegel

Still as a silk screen I wait, I wait,
invisible, part of the furniture,
for the ambling fly or worm,
the Monarch just alighting,
the beetle dark under its armor.
On the altar of my arms, I offer up
whatever wanders by. In love
I am insatiable, will take
my mate's head in his electric need
and devour it, swallowing his body
almost as an afterthought;
then, absent-mindedly,
moving stiff and brittle as a tree,
go propagate my kind.

Moth at My Window

Richard Aldridge

Against my pane
He beats a rapid
Pitapat
In trying to reach
The desk lamp lit
In front of me.
Wing flurries spent,
He crawls and toils
This way and that,
His whole self bound
To pierce the veil
He cannot see.

The glance I turn
On him, light
Spreading still across
My page, is one
Of interest in
The company.
Whatever time

I take to watch
Will be no loss
From my own toils
To pierce the veil
I cannot see.

Garden Spider

Richard Foerster

Argiope bruennichi

An orbweaver, adrift among
the hosta's spent stalks, black
and brilliant-banded gold, dead-

center in a mist of silks and two
zigzag vertical rays strung as luminous
warning to any flying bird, hovered

last evening, head earthward, her legs
poised to set the web trembling to a blur
each time I crouched to watch, spell-

bound and snared with the thought
that here's the perfect fretwork
to grace a backyard garden. Now

this morning I see she's consumed
each filament, digested the indispensible
proteins to respin the entire design

somewhere away from my quisitive gaze.
What must I admire, left with empty
space: an unbending mind

fixed on private workings, or the way
the very fabric of a world
can be chewed up for weaving again?

Lost Graveyards

Elizabeth Coatsworth

In Maine the dead
melt into the forest
like Indians, or, rather,
in Maine the forests shadow round the dead
until the dead are indistinguishably mingled
with trees; while underground,
roots and bones intertwine,
and above earth
the tilted gravestones, lichen-covered, too,
shine faintly out from among pines and birches,
burial stones and trunks
growing together
above the lattices of roots and bones.
Now is the battle over,
the harsh struggle
between man and the forest.
While they lived,
these men and women fought the encroaching trees,
hacked them with axes,
severed them with saws,
burned them in fires,
pushed them back and back

to their last lairs among the shaggy hills,
while the green fields lay tame about the houses.
Living they fought the wild,
but dead, they rested,
and the wild softly, silently, secretly,
returned. In Maine
the dead sooner or later feel the hug of rootlets,
and shadowy branches closing out the sun.

Gulls in Wind

Betsy Sholl

Bedraggled feathers like bonnets
that would fly off if they weren't strapped,
kazoo-voiced, a chorus of crying dolphins
or rusty sirens a speck of dust could set off —
these raucous gleaners milling around

pick up and discard, now a Q-tip,
now a shred of lettuce or cellophane,
a cigarette butt one holds a second
as if he really might smoke. One drags
an old condom, one spots a good crumb

and walk-runs, squawks everyone else away.
But it's just a dried scrap of weed he'll toss back,
grist for the next fool's expectation.
Still, a loud alpha catches wind,
scoots over to check it out. Shove off,

he screeches, this is my no-good, barren,
motel-infested spit of sand — on which
he neither toils nor spins, but grubs all day

on webbed feet and clever back-hinged knees,
now skittishly sidestepping a gusty

piece of plastic blown against his legs,
hopping to get it off, now shaking it
once or twice to make sure it's worthless
before he turns his face to the wind,
letting it smooth his fine fractious feathers.

The Habitation

Lewis Turco

There is no way out.
Now the windows have begun
to cloud over: cobwebs, dust.
The stairs and floors are unstable —
the hours nibble the foundations.

In the bedrooms, sheets
have begun to yellow, spreads
to fray. Coverlets have worn
to the colors of late autumn,
thin as a draft sifting at the sill.

On the kitchen floor
crumbs and rinds lie recalling
the old feasts. In the larder
preserves rust among speckled jars;
the bins yawn; shadow sates the cupboards.

The fire has been damped
at the hearth: its bed of ash
sinks in pit-holes over brick.
The ceiling snows on the carpet —
Rejoice! Rejoice! The house is failing!

The Last Lamp-Lighters

Kenneth Rosen

I saw the last lamp-lighters! Patrolling
      The dusk, looking for gas-lamps
Whose lights had gone out. Each held a pole
Forked for lifting the frail pearl-tinted bowl,
And one with a small wheel and flint for casting

A spark. Did all lamps need to be lit? Or just
      Those doused by raindrops or errant drafts?
They seemed sad, these doomed men who knew
How to give fog its soft perfume, and the facts
Of our life their necessary, tender, but fatal glow.

Closing Time

Dave Morrison

The bartender has just announced last call.
It feels like bedtime did when we were young;
we act surprised, and then we act appalled.
It's much too soon, and we aren't nearly done,
but just like then, no matter what we say,
we have to move along, we cannot stay.

The bouncer has a sideshow barker's call:
"Come on people, drink 'em up, let's go,
it's hotel-motel time, the clock on the wall
says that this bar ain't open any more. . ."
When lights come on it's unnerving to see
the club in all its tattered misery.

The soundman coils the cables on the stage
just like a sailor making fast his ship.
The weary waitress starts to feel her age
and rubs her temples while she counts her tips.
The barback lugs the cases up the stairs
and fills the coolers with tomorrow's beers.

The sadness of anonymous goodbyes —
we drain our drinks and shuffle out the door
to make our way back to whatever lives
we left to come here several hours before.
Unfinished business always seems to shape
our attempts at transformation and escape.

Changes of Heart

The Net

Peter Harris

I saw the black maid park the Cadillac
in the lot of the Indian Harbor Yacht Club.
When she hefted the first huge silver tray
of delicacies for that evening's soiree
on her boss' yacht, I offered to help.

No, she said, in her starched gray uniform
on orders from her employer. The launch man
in wrinkled khakis and a black cap with gold
braided on the bill, told her no, she couldn't
ride the launch. Against Club rules.

But I am just bringing out the food, she said.
Everyone looked at the ground. The launch man
and the maid in their uniforms with strict orders,
me, at twelve, with my marlin spike and stopwatch,
still learning the lines, the tactics of yachting.

I'd never been so close to a black person.
I could see the whites of her eyes flash.
She was caught. He was caught. I
didn't know that I'd been caught. I couldn't
feel the hook that pinned my tongue to my cheek.

But stepping aboard the launch, I felt the net,
woven so carefully by so many hands,
the seamless, almost miraculously strong,
transparent canopy that would keep everyone
in Greenwich exquisitely and forever in place.

Making the Turn

Sarah Jane Woolf-Wade

There comes a time
with dependable rhythm
every year
late in August
when the wind turns around,
blows in air from the north
to chill the bay
and the year turns its face
away from summer.

Monarch butterflies
ripple down to zinnias that bend
toward late afternoon sun,
bank their wings
and lean into the last leg
of their unavoidable flight plan.

Sometime in every life
there comes that inevitable turn
when we face away. . .
I can't be sure when that moment was for me.

The Geese

May Sarton

The geese honked overhead.
I ran to catch the skein
To watch them as they fled
In a long wavering line.

I caught my breath, alone,
Abandoned like a lover
With winter at the bone
To see the geese go over.

It happens every year
And every year some woman
Haunted by loss and fear
Must take it as an omen,

Must shiver as she stands
Watching the wild geese go,
With sudden empty hands
Before the cruel snow.

Some woman every year
Must catch her breath and weep
With so much wildness near
At all she cannot keep.

Inland

Edna St. Vincent Millay

People that build their houses inland,
    People that buy a plot of ground
Shaped like a house, and build a house there,
    Far from the sea-board, far from the sound

Of water sucking the hollow ledges,
    Tons of water striking the shore, —
What do they long for, as I long for
    One salt smell of the sea once more?

People the waves have not awakened,
    Spanking the boats at the harbour's head,
What do they long for, as I long for, —
    Starting up in my inland bed,

Beating the narrow walls, and finding
    Neither a window nor a door,
Screaming to God for death by drowning, —
    One salt taste of the sea once more?

Hearing Your Words, and Not a Word Among Them

Edna St. Vincent Millay

Hearing your words, and not a word among them
Tuned to my liking, on a salty day
When inland woods were pushed by winds that flung them
Hissing to leeward like a ton of spray;
I thought how off Matinicus the tide
Came pounding in, came running though the Gut,
While from the Rock the morning whistle cried,
And children whimpered and the doors blew shut;
There in the autumn when the men go forth,
In gardens stripped and scattered, peering north,
With dahlia tubers dripping from the hand:
The wind of their endurance, driving south,
Flattened your words against your speaking mouth.

Humane Society

Bruce Spang

The neighbor's pup,
wanting in,
won't let up.
Yelp. Yelp. Yelp.
This, the fourth night
of its desperation.

Our two cats huddle
at the open window
pretending to be sympathetic.
Downstairs, the cuckoo pleads
its shrill three-stress call.

I can remember,
shivering in my pajamas,
calling out, again and again,
Sandy, Sandy, Sandy,
drifting into blackness.
Leave it alone, My wife would intone.
Let it learn.

But it was not the dog I was calling,
not then, when my marriage
could be counted in the three-word
sentences we barked between us.
It was my wanting out, there
on the porch in the cold,
waiting to hear how far my voice
could carry across night fields.

Reuben Bright

Edwin Arlington Robinson

Because he was a butcher and thereby
Did earn an honest living (and did right),
I would not have you think that Reuben Bright
Was any more a brute than you or I;
For when they told him that his wife must die,
He stared at them, and shook with grief and fright,
And cried like a great baby half that night,
And made the women cry to see him cry.

And after she was dead, and he had paid
The singers and the sexton and the rest,
He packed a lot of things that she had made
Most mournfully away in an old chest
Of hers, and put some chopped-up cedar boughs
In with them, and tore down the slaughter house.

Sudden Death

Linda Buckmaster

You were an electric current leaping
between contact points, living always
so bright, so hot until
that moment

you shorted out, caught fire, and
bursting into white flames,
consumed yourself
in light and heat, leaving us
the still warm ashes of an afterlife.

January

Linda Buckmaster

The other night, I saw you
as moonlight coming in
the west window of the kitchen.
Fourteen years in this house and I never
before saw the moon coming in that particular window.
Perhaps it's that we never stayed up so late,
at least not on bright nights in winter when
the low-slung moon moves around
the corner of the house and into the side yard. Or
perhaps it's just that I never noticed before now. Now

I'm often up very late, alone,
so that night I saw you softly spreading
across the dark countertop and burnished surface
of the stove — a triangle of light — and
I lowered my face and kissed you.

A Little Bit of Timely Advice

Mekeel McBride

Time you put on blue
shoes, high-heeled, sequined,
took yourself out dancing.

You been spending too much
time crying salty
dead-fish lakes into soupspoons,

holding look-alike contests
with doom. Baby, you
need to be moving. Ruin

ruins itself, no use unplanting
what's left of your garden.
Crank up the old radio

into lion-looking-for-food
music; or harmonica, all indigo,
breathing up sunrise. Down

and out's just another opinion
on up and over. You say
you got no makings

for a song? Sing anyway.
Best music's the stuff comes
rising out of nothing.

Early Morning Trumpet

George V. Van Deventer

for Gabe

On occasion, leaving the barn
after milking, I'd hear
my neighbor's son down the valley,
across the stream, play
his trumpet as if he were thinking out loud, moving
in the privacy of his thoughts.
I'd stop as if it were a call to prayer
and follow his flight,
as I would follow a nuthatch
piping from tree to tree —
a personal song
unfolding around me.

April Prayer

Stuart Kestenbaum

Just before the green begins there is the hint of green
a blush of color, and the red buds thicken
the ends of the maple's branches and everything
is poised before the start of a new world,
which is really the same world
just moving forward from bud
to flower to blossom to fruit
to harvest to sweet sleep, and the roots
await the next signal, every signal
every call a miracle and the switchboard
is lighting up and the operators are
standing by in the pledge drive we've
all been listening to: Go make the call.

Transportation

Kristen Lindquist

Everyone in O'Hare is happy today.
Sun shines benevolently
onto glorious packaged snack foods
and racks of Bulls T-shirts.
My plane was twenty minutes early.
Even before I descend into the trippy light show
of the walkway between terminals,
I am ecstatic. I can't stop smiling.
On my flight we saw Niagara Falls
and Middle America green and gold below.
Passengers thanked the pilot for his smooth landing
with such gratitude that I too
thanked him, with sudden and wholehearted sincerity.
A group of schoolchildren passes on the escalator,
and I want to ask where they're going.
Tell me your story, I want to say.
This is life in motion.
A young couple embraces tearfully at a gate;
she's leaving, he's not.
How can I bring this new self back to you, intact?
He yells to her departing back,

"Hey, I like the way you move!"
Any kind of love seems possible.
We walk through this light together.
So what if it's an airport?
So what if it won't last?

Nude

Robert Siegel

Content in her skin she does not challenge
the blue shadow cast over much of her body,
waiting in the shade like a center of gravity,
so full, even the trees have travelled too far.

Her breasts steal the wind with surprise,
promise long savannahs of discovery
beyond the trembling compass of a flower
or tuft of weeds agog with her sweet breath.

I stand in this museum looking,
blood sagging to my fingers and toes.
The sun is coming at me through the wall.
Clothes could never touch her, this one, put
beyond the night whisper and morning's flat red mouth
into the first turning of the light.

The Alligator's Hum

Kenneth Rosen

To allure an alligator lady so she'll allow him
To fertilize her eggs before she buries them
In her sand nest, the male alligator
  Hums in a swamp pond like a kid in a bathtub.
It hums like a foghorn: *Hummmmmm!* And raises
Queer geysers of water by his torso's profound
Vibrations, these inverted, fragile, almost crystal
Chandeliers his obligatto of amor. I have tried this
  On dates without knowing what I was doing:
Hummmmmm! My date pretended she didn't know
  What I was doing either and would ask,
"Are you all right?" *Hmmmmmm!* I'd echo,

Something below my solar plexus now governing
My lowest, reptilian, ganglion brain. But I swear,
  Like people who claim they can't understand poetry,
She knew what it meant for the hum of the body
To dominate mind. It meant please admire

My wet inverted chandeliers, which translates
Like all poetry too, into alligator: "You can get me,
  If you let me, you grinning, beautiful
primordial swampwater creature you!" Then their tails
  Slap the water with a belly whomp.
They thrash like mad, almost invincible — though the human
  Eye is never naked — and then it's over.

Ball Smacks Mouth, Splits Lip

Bob MacLaughlin

Marietta Mansfield came walking up
the driveway while I was playing catch
with her brother on the grass,
so I, who had it bad for Marietta Mansfield,
looked over at her an instant before the ball
smacked me in the mouth, splitting my upper lip.

Their mother took me to Dr. Waddle, who stitched
the pieces back together well enough
for Marietta Mansfield to kiss me on that mouth
a month later in a dark ping-pong room.

The next morning I went away to summer camp,
where I played on the baseball team
and wrote letters to Marietta Mansfield
every day, and she to me, until hers stopped,
whereupon I fell into a terrible batting slump.

After camp I went off to high school in the next town,
but Marietta Mansfield was still in eighth grade
so I hardly ever saw her, ignored her when I did,

said snide things she could overhear
so she would feel as bad as I felt.

Years later, when I found out our letters
had been shortstopped by her mother,
I felt even worse.

Sandwiches

Pam Burr Smith

When I was young
My mother made me sandwiches for lunch
Butter on one slice of bread
Mayo on the other
Lettuce and tomato
Bologna or salami
Two slices always
Or tuna salad or meatloaf

These were big thick sandwiches
That could fall apart

Not like those one slice of bread
One slice of ham
One slice of bread sandwiches
The cool kids had

I wanted everything the cool kids had
And I wanted their dry little sandwiches, too

Mine were so obviously made by a mother
Clumsy in their over-love
Every taste and vitamin she could pack into them
Every morning too full too full
I needed two napkins to eat them

Not like the cool kids
Who could hold a neat little sandwich
In one hand
While mine dribbled love
Down my arm

The Goldfish

Mekeel McBride

It was a feeder, which means it was supposed
to get fed to something bigger like a barracuda.
But I put the ten-cent comet in clean water
with enough food, no predators, and it grew
into a radiant glider full of happy appetite.

That was the truth of it for a long time and then
the fish, for no reason that I could see, suddenly
curled upside down into a red question mark.
Now, its golden scales drop off like sequins
from a museum dress and its mouth forms over

and over the same empty O. Though I wish to,
there's no way to free it, not even for a second,
from its own slow death. You say this fish is the least
of it, that I'd better start worrying about what's
really wrong: a child chained somewhere

in a basement, starving; the droop-eyed man,
cooking up, in a cast-iron kettle, germ stew
that will end the world. But that's exactly what I said.
The golden thing is dying right on the other side
of the glass; I can see it and there's nothing I can do.

The Plymouth on Ice

Thomas R. Moore

On frigid January nights we'd
take my 'forty-eight Plymouth onto
the local reservoir, lights off
to dodge the cops, take turns

holding long manila lines in pairs
behind the car, cutting colossal
loops and swoons across
the crackly range of ice. Oh

God, did we have fun! At ridges
and fissures we careened,
tumbled onto each other, the girls
yelping, splayed out on all fours,

and sometimes we heard groans
deep along the fracture lines as
we spun off in twos, to paw, clumsy,
under parkas, never thinking of

love's falls or how thin ice
would ease us into certain death.
No, death was never on our minds,
we were eighteen, caterwauling

under our own moon that
warded off cops and
front-page stories of six kids
slipping under the fickle surface.

The Hands

Bruce Guernsey

The only time we touch now
is in our sleep, as if our hands,
finding each other,
have lives of their own.

Joined to our surprise every morning,
they are full of longing,
like a one-armed man
trying to pray.

We pull them apart
starting the day, yours
to your work, mine to mine:
purses, pockets, change.

How they love the night,
the cool of linen, the underside
of pillows — sneaking out,
meeting without us in the dark.

Theirs is a language we've forgotten,
a way of speaking now their own:
touching, whispering,
making plans.

Divorce

Donald Crane

She got the path to the spring house
through the asters and fireweed
and the orange "touch me not."

The grey smudges that are deer
at the far edge of the pasture at dusk.

The broad leaves of the rhubarb plant
where early in the morning
the swallowtail butterflies lie
motionless with their wings spread
to dry.

Redtail hawks overhead; jays fussing
in the apple orchard gone wild.

And from the kitchen window; the faint
haze in September over Tunk Mountain
20 miles away.

I got pigeons and starlings in the Bangor
city park, and a job stacking boxes
at the Mall.

Feed My Birds

Elizabeth McFarland

Feed my birds,
But not the whitethroat in his cage of air!
Feed robin, hawk,
The attendant flock
Of rooftree birds, and birds of prey or prayer;
But not the lost love calling, calling there.

At that wild voice
Trees touch their tips together and rejoice,
Rising full-leaved through waterfalls of sound.
That evergreen lament
Beyond all words has sent
Touch as soft as moss on woodland limbs unbound.

O feed them, scatter seed upon the ground!
Feed homing dove and jay,
Chickadees in black beret,
Feed simple starling, thrush, and small-shawled wren;
But sparrow, the white-throated one,
Feed not again!

Hummingbird

Ellen M. Taylor

A hummingbird's heart
beats 250 times per minute
when resting
and 1200 times while feeding.
A surprise can trigger
cardiac arrest,
as his tiny heart
cannot withstand
further stress.

I mourn
the ruby-throated juvenile
anxiously feeding in the phlox
this still September morning.
His whirring startled me
while I knelt to deadhead pansies —
I swatted at the sound,
and he fell.

Hen

Ellen M. Taylor

How does she do it, create such perfect
spheres within her feathered body? Every
twenty-four hours she leaves us, still warm,
an umber shell, inside it a yolk, ochre
and richer than butter, nested in white clear
as rainwater. She coos and clucks with content.

Loon Return

Carol Willette Bachofner

Long ribbons of loons
descend through a cleft
in the spreading morning;
resplendent in formal attire,
they dip into icy meltwater ponds.
Beautiful, eerie laughter heralds
oncoming spring, breaks the boreal
winter silence with its return.

Regret

Bob Brooks

It's like skipping a stone —
one thing reminds me of another.
And when the stone sinks,
I don't go after it.

I don't go after it.
But when the stone sinks,
it reminds me of another.

Another regret
like a skipping stone
I don't go after —

another stone,
sinking.

Snap

Bob Brooks

Poor mousie
living for months

on toilet paper
from the linen closet

one day finds bagels
and English muffins
in a kitchen cupboard

thinks she's died
and gone to heaven

yep

He Sees the Future

Dave Morrison

Her fingers flutter light, like butterflies.
The bass notes belt him like a boxer's gloves —
amazing octave leaps for such small hands.
She's pretty, sure, and young but that's not why
he stands and stares and falls mutely in love.

Her body and the bass's form a curve
that follows from her right hand to her left.
She looks as if she's watching weather come
or trying to place a stranger in a crowd.
She lets herself become lost in the sound,
and now she's trying to find her way back home.

She doesn't seem concerned about the band
or audience; she plays for someone else
he remembers when his playing caused a stir.
Now that seems a long, long time ago.
He feels like a distracted dinosaur
watching the approaching meteor.

Musician

Louise Bogan

Where have these hands been,
By what delayed,
That so long stayed
Apart from the thin

Strings which they now grace
With their lonely skill?
Music and their cool will
At last interlace.

Now with great ease, and slow,
The thumb, the finger, the strong
Delicate hand plucks the long
String it was born to know.

And, under the palm, the string
Sings as it wished to sing.

Today, the Traffic Signals All Changed for Me

Martin Steingesser

It's all language, I am thinking
on my way over the drawbridge to South Portland,
driving into a wishbone blue, autumn sky, maple
red, aspen yellow — oaks, evergreens
stretching out in sunlight. Isn't this all
message and sign, singing to us?
When I open ears, listen with eyes
wide open, the world tumbles in, suddenly
a rush through my body, how tires zummmmm
across a bridge grating, sending vibratos
along limbs, out fingers
and toes. Even these dead things
we make: cement walkways,
macadam streets, all our brick and steel
and rubber, even these are alive. Sometimes
I feel so empty. Today, I am filling up, the way
this Indian Summer morning keeps fattening
on sunlight, feelings, words frothing like yeast.
Blue sky rises in my blood, geese
and monarchs migrating through; my love's an open field,
meadows of goldfinch, Anne's lace, new moon

and crow laughing. . . Tornadoes
collapse in a breath, oceans curl at my toes, galaxies
exploding in my heart. Am I going loco? I pull over
onto the roadside, cars and trucks whizzing by.
I can't get places I thought I was going. I think of old Walt,
quadrupeds and birds stucco'd all over. Why not?
And you, too, Allen, gay, locomotive sunflower laureate,
both of you, among the leaves, in your all-star colors,
hitting all the curves, belting poems
out of the century. O look! — this is what's happening.

Last Writes

Carl Little

*"I tinker with most of my poems even after publication. I expect to be
revising in my coffin as it is being lowered into the ground."*

— *Charles Simic*

At the wake for the ex-U.S. poet laureate
at the Hotel Fin du Monde someone swore
he heard a scratching sound in the casket

and later, as we wedged the box into
a rocky corner of a New Hampshire bone orchard,
one of the pall bearers, a pallid poet with

acute hearing, caught the sibilant sound
of the words being crossed out — "kissing"
substituted for "praying," perhaps, or

"lover" for "beloved" — the gentle rub
of eraser, the whisper of a breath
to remove residue from the paper

and the click of the miner's lamp
Simic insisted wearing on his head
in lieu of the standard issue laurel wreath.

The World and
Back Again

What Positions Do They and We Assume in the Encapsulated Stillness?

John Tagliabue

While

somewhere in a capsule deep in the sea
off the Florida coast
seven visitors to the earth who planned to
visit outer space
lie dead with their advanced technological gadgets
and once active
mysterious eyes, all kinds of scientists and many
argumentative committees
discuss in details the possible causes of the Challenger's
explosion, flaming
demise into fish-wandering seas. Octopus nearby,
and dead sea captains,
ships like old cultures gone to the bottom. The many
slightly alive
statisticians argue and probe and computers they think
are at their advanced
command. How silent they are, the sky dreamers, those
children in the womb
of the metal.

For the Falling Man

Annie Farnsworth

I see you again and again
tumbling out of the sky,
in your slate-gray suit and pressed white shirt.
At first I thought you were debris
from the explosion, maybe gray plaster wall
or fuselage but then I realized
that people were leaping.
I know who you are, I know
there's more to you than just this image
on the news, this ragdoll plummeting —
I know you were someone's lover, husband,
daddy. Last night you read stories
to your children, tucked them in, then curled into sleep
next to your wife. Perhaps there was small
sleepy talk of the future. Then,
before your morning coffee had cooled
you'd come to this; a choice between fire
or falling.
How feeble these words, billowing

in this aftermath, how ineffectual
this utterance of sorrow. We can see plainly
it's hopeless, even as the words trail from our mouths
— but we can't help ourselves — how I wish
we could trade them for something
that could really have caught you.

United States

Phillip Booth

All right, we are two nations.

Immaculate floors, ceilings broken
only by skylights. The insulated
walls, the soundless heat; and hidden
everywhere, a fan for every odor.

Of our two nations
that is one.

>   And you who will not
read this

>   presume you know the other.

Airfield

Robert Siegel

All day the great planes gingerly descend
an invisible staircase, holding up
their skirts and dignity like great ladies
in technicolor histories, or reascend,
their noses needling upward like a compass
into a wild blue vacuum,
leaving everything in confusion behind:

In some such self-deceiving light as this
we'll view the air force base when moved away
from where its sleepless eye revolves all night.
We'll smile and recollect it conversationally —
tell with what ease the silver planes dropped down
or how they, weightless, rose above
our roof. We'll pass it with a sugar and cream,

forever sheltered from this moment's sick
surprise that we have lived with terror, with pride,
the wounded god circling the globe, never resting,
that in the morning and the evening we have heard
his cry, have seen him drag his silver wings
whining with anguish like a huge
fly seeking to lay its deadly eggs.

Night Patrol

Bruce Guernsey

My father never slept real well after the war
and as my mother tells, he woke in fear
so deep, so far away, he seemed to stare
straight out at nothing she could see or hear.

Or worse — she wraps her robe around her, remembering —
he'd sit there grinning, bolt upright beside her,
this mad look on his face, the bed springs quivering
with some hilarity the night had whispered.

And once, "He did this, your father, I swear he did —
he must have been still dreaming, rest his soul —
he tried to close my frightened eyes, my lids,
to thumb them shut like he was on patrol

the way he'd learned so they would sleep, the dead.
And then he blessed himself and bowed his head."

Unknown Algonquin Females, Circa 1800s

Carol Willette Bachofner

They dug up my grandmother, moved her
to the museum. No one stopped them.
I had no say. De-recognized by government,
filed at the BIA under "I" (*Indian, former*),
she's been reduced to anthropology, curated
by bureaucrats, her bones on display
with the bones of a woman from an enemy tribe:
(*Unknown Algonquin Females, Circa 1800s*)
No one sang a travel song for her to ease her bones
along the way; no giveaway, no mourning strings
to soften the sorrow. I have watched their grandmas
prayed and cried into the ground, names cut
into marble, bodies preserved under stones safe
behind iron gates. The governor's announcement claims
today: *There are no Abenaki Indians left in Vermont.*

Nobody at Treblinka

Thomas Carper

"Sie waren nicht ein kleiner Mann."
            — Film director Claude Lanzmann
                to a former Nazi official

But keep the scale in mind. What single man
Could undertake that kind of enterprise
When each day trains from half of Europe ran
Into the camp? The prisoners swarmed like flies
Onto the platforms. Hundreds did their jobs
Of keeping books, processing and selecting,
Or guarding work brigades, or moving mobs
Into the chambers...cleaning...disinfecting.
You see, with those large numbers, no one said,
"X is responsible." We were a team
Handling the hordes — the living, and the dead.
Mine was a minor function. Do I seem
Like someone who would cause such sufferings?
I was a nobody. Nobody does those things.

To Jesus on His Birthday

Edna St. Vincent Millay

For this your mother sweated in the cold,
For this you bled upon the bitter tree:
A yard of tinsel ribbon bought and sold;
A paper wreath; a day at home for me.
The merry bells ring out, the people kneel;
Up goes the man of God before the crowd;
With voice of honey and with eyes of steel
He drones your humble gospel to the proud.
Nobody listens. Less than the wind that blows
Are all your words to us you died to save.
O Prince of Peace! O Sharon's dewy Rose!
How mute you lie within your vaulted grave.
The stone the angel rolled away with tears
Is back upon your mouth these thousand years.

From the Toy Box

Nancy Henry

God
they sent me to tell you
none of us can help it.
Can't operate correctly,
can't fly, won't wind up,
can't even make a start
for the tops of those clouds.
So many pieces melted,
bent, skewed, pocked,
utterly undermined with rust.

What we want to know:
when this ends,
how will you decide
which ones of us
are most broken,
how will you choose
which ones of us
to throw away?

Out Here

Robin Merrill

I know why he killed himself.
You know, the old man
who spent thirty years
trying to break out of prison
and his last two
aching to get back in.
I know him, how he missed
that cold comfort of gray.
I too, have seen colors to be scary.
I know why he carved his name
in the headboard at the boarding house
before he swallowed the stolen pills.
For thirty years they barked his name.
He hasn't heard it since. After living
the same day over and over,
regimen and routine,
now he wakes without schedule.
There are no friends here.
There is no family.
He left all of that behind.
Though he didn't know it then,
prison gave him purpose.
It's lonely out here.

Free Agent

Marija Sanderling

He shoots baskets
The empty lot
The netless hoop
Suspended like a halo
His daily routine
Sometimes with others
Mostly alone
To shoot and dribble
Like the players on tv
He's a free agent
Who dropped out of school
So even the gym teacher
Can't tell him
If he's any good.
Three hours a day
No traveling
No transitions
Just free throws and slam dunks
And all it's gotten him
Is a 90% success rate
And a view of the city
Through the chain-link fence.

To the Infinitesimal

Betsy Sholl

I opened a holy book, hoping to find
the part about turning the other cheek,
and out you flew, hovering dot

smaller than a comma, winged inkling.
Were you late when names were given out,
an afterthought, spittle from a cough

at the end of creation? Feeling you
graze my check, I lunged like a clumsy golem,
but you gave me the slip.

How can anything so small have a will,
a want, the wits to flee two clapped hands?
In a time revving for war, with experts

stoking the engines, insisting necessity,
you're a nil, a naught, a nuisance to ignore,
not one of mystery's vexing ellipses. . .

If your wings whir, if you buzz at all,
it's below our hearing, little serif
broken off some word in holy writ

to drift among us, inaudible
argument illustrating creation's
fondness for every last tittle and jot.

Death and the Turtle

May Sarton

I watched the turtle dwindle day by day,
Get more remote, lie limp upon my hand;
When offered food he turned his head away;
The emerald shell grew soft. Quite near the end
Those withdrawn paws stretched out to grasp
His long head in a poignant dying gesture.
It was so strangely like a human clasp,
My heart cracked for the brother creature.

I buried him, wrapped in a lettuce leaf,
The vivid eye sunk inward, a dull stone.
So this was it, the universal grief;
Each bears his own end knit up in the bone.
Where are the dead? we ask, as we hurtle
Toward the dark, part of this strange creation,
One with each limpet, leaf, and smallest turtle —
Cry out for life, cry out in desperation!

Who will remember you when I have gone,
My darling ones, or who remember me?
Only in our wild hearts the dead live on.
Yet these frail engines bound to mystery

Break the harsh turn of all creation's wheel,
For we remember China, Greece, and Rome,
Our mothers and our fathers, and we steal
From death itself rich store, and bring it home.

Nature

Henry Wadsworth Longfellow

As a fond mother, when the day is o'er,
   Leads by the hand her little child to bed,
   Half willing, half reluctant to be led,
   And leave his broken playthings on the floor,
Still gazing at them through the open door,
   Nor wholly reassured and comforted
   By promises of others in their stead,
   Which, though more splendid, may not please him more;

So Nature deals with us, and takes away
   Our playthings one by one, and by the hand
   Leads us to rest so gently, that we go
Scarce knowing if we wish to go or stay,
   Being too full of sleep to understand
   How far the unknown transcends the what we know.

Question in a Field

Louise Bogan

Pasture, stone wall, and steeple,
What most perturbs the mind:
The heart-rending homely people,
Or the horrible beautiful kind?

To an Artist, to Take Heart

Louise Bogan

Slipping in blood, by his own hand, through pride,
Hamlet, Othello, Coriolanus fall.
Upon his bed, however, Shakespeare died,
Having endured them all.

Salt to the Brain
(In Praise of Poets)
David Moreau

As a rule we are not the brain surgeons
or the bridge builders. We did not figure
how to make water flow in a pipe
or keep airplanes stable in flight.
Instead, we stood in a circle and chanted,
"All praise to the most beautiful bridge,"
then walked across it.

As a rule we do not meet the payroll
or keep the factories open.
Others figured how enzymes work
and built hydraulic brakes.
Instead, we were the ones at the machines
whose idea it was to sing, "Happy Birthday,"
or "Nobody Knows the Trouble I've Seen."

In this world the moneychangers change money.
The nurses nurse and the lawyers lawyer.
My mother feeds the stray cats that come

to the screen door of her house in Marion Oaks.
The orange tiger has a nasty scratch.
The poets take note,
add this small pinch of salt to the brain,
our gift to the taste of existence.

Where Inspiration Has Learned a Thing or Two

Mekeel McBride

From the trees because they are the true intuitives.
Palm readers of sunlight and storm, calm interpreters
for any kind of wind, doing most of the detective work
on shooting stars and aurora borealis. Their easy come,
easy go romances with migrating birds scarcely bear
recording and not even the quick cinema jump cuts
from summer to snow bother them. Even if there is snow,
temperature in the minus numbers, something continues
to live, invisible, at the core. Looking at the trees, you might
see in the bare branches only the bones of Babayaga's hand
or the possibility of kindling for your wood stove, owl haven,
or a kind of living elegy blessed on the highest branch
by one thin crow. Of course you could be wrong. What
inspiration looks like is never really what it is.

Spring Thaw

Ruth F. Guillard

Night, early April
White rivers of rain, snowmelt
Roar over the rocks
Scouring the steep slopes
Tripping over grey boulders
Hillsides echoing

Every spring I wait
For this sweet sound of release
The earth rejoicing.

Growing Lettuce

Henry Braun

I have broken soil
and run a line in the blackness with my finger
and dropped the flea-like seeds in
too thickly.

Even so, even so,
the lettuce comes, standing room only,
as a favor to a first try
and is a shy green.

Zones of Peeper

Carl Little

Driving home from a party, parsing
conversations, car windows down
to greet first real summer heat,
we pass through zones of peeper —

not song, not chorus, though
scientists no doubt find pattern
in the high-pitched whatever it is.
Nor peep, which reminds you of

silly chicks falling over each other
in an incubator. Every moist venue
between Pretty Marsh and Somesville,
every hundred yards brings

this antic singing, somewhat
alien in tone, magical too,
like fireflies but auditory,
not synthesized but a perfect

cacophony of the higher ranges,
tiny frogs doing their spring thing,
flinging music into dank milieu
of pond edge and marsh, inspiring

a certain joy in our recap of the evening
as if every fault could be forgiven
when you consider the rest of the world
wild and wet and flipping out.

Fiddleheads

Richard Foerster

Only the first scrolls inscripted
with the long winter's undeciphered
lore, only the tight-harnessed
coils volting up fully
charged from peaty earth would do:

tiny crosiers straining to hook
the sky; spring's furled lace —
wings before the sun had a chance
to spirit them with flight. Arrested

potential I demanded with each
flick of my pruning knife, not
woodland crofts feathered wide
in August with spore-laden tracery.

How the future seemed to lie
there before me, curled and delectable.
Already the virgin oil sizzled
in my mind till I was sure
the skillet would whisper hosannas.

My Hairy Legs

Mariana S. Tupper

My hairy legs say No to sheer pantyhose
accompanied by stiff pumps and hard soles.
No to razors, depilatories and electrolysis.

They resent hours in the bathroom
yanking on fabric strips
and wiping up little hairs in the tub.

My hairy legs take a stand against propriety.

They say Yes to shorts,
Yes please to stockings with crazy stripes.

My hairy legs are happy to wear pants,
and gowns on formal occasions,

though they long for the moment
when the party is over and they can kick up
their heels and feel the wind in their hair.

Spring Cleaning

Ellen M. Taylor

Why are there no poems of the joy
of vacuum cleaning after a long

winter? Of the pleasure of pulling
the couch back, sucking up cobwebs, dead

flies, candy cane wrappers, cookie crumbs?
The sun rises earlier now, flooding

the room with daffodil light, enough
to see long unseen clumps of dog hair,

wood ash, needles from holiday greens.
The vacuum crackles over a spot

of gravelly dirt, until at last
the carpet pile is clean, floorboards gleam.

Then, the bliss when the machine is pressed off,
no sound left but the tick, tick of the clock.

A Parrot

May Sarton

My parrot is emerald green,
His tail feathers, marine.
He bears an orange half-moon
Over his ivory beak.
He must be believed to be seen,
This bird from a Rousseau wood.
When the urge is on him to speak,
He becomes too true to be good.

He uses his beak like a hook
To lift himself up with or break
Open a sunflower seed,
And his eye, in a bold white ring,
Has a lapidary look.
What a most astonishing bird,
Whose voice when he chooses to sing
Must be believed to be heard.

That stuttered staccato scream
Must be believed not to seem
The shriek of a witch in the room.

But he murmurs some muffled words
(Like someone who talks through a dream)
When he sits in the window and sees
To to-and-fro wings of wild birds
In the leafless improbable trees.

Spooked Moose

Douglas Woody Woodsum

Like a real bull in a bullfight, the full-grown moose
Lowered his head and ripped through my neighbor's laundry, pinned
To the line from the house corner to the apple tree.

And like a bride with a twenty-foot train, it dragged the line
And the clothes across my neighbor's lawn, leaving a wake
Of clothespins, jeans, tee shirts, and boxer shorts every few yards.

Then, like a moose in a panic because it has rope
And clothing tangled about its horns and more rope and clothes flapping
About its torso and rear legs, very like such a moose,

It lowered its head again and charged through the old barbed wire
Pasture fence, snapping the rotten fenceposts off at ground level,
Dragging and, finally, snapping, the rusty wires of a forgotten farm.

And then like a fearful beast learning fear for the first time,
It picked up speed as a bedsheet flopped onto its face
and three or four dragging fenceposts barked its rear ankles and shins.

It tripped and fell breaking through the fence again on the far
Side of the field, but struggled up once more to crash
Into the undergrowth and disappear amid the trees.

Lastly, like stunned townspeople in the wake of a twister,
My neighbor and I picked up the strewn pieces of clothing
As we followed tracks, like post-holes, into the dented woods.

New England Asters

Lynn Ascrizzi

They're firing purple from the rock wall,
shouting hurrahs amid gloriosas,
towering on leggy stalks
near the rose trellis, before the frost.

The dames are taking over.
Fringy and sticky, drunk with nectar,
they lean and swagger,
staging a revolution.

Volunteers from last year's seeds
spring up near the house,
and new forces bivouac
down the long dirt drive,
ready to occupy the roadside
past the mailbox.

Shovel in hand, I am fully enlisted
in the cause of late bloomers.
I transplant rootstock,

shake out new progeny,
post ensigns amid the wan and cheerless,
marshal troops down desolate hollows,
seed my universe with stars.

They All Come Back

Sarah Jane Woolf-Wade

The girl who shone in Broadway shows
was born here in the village on Fourth of July
and a Rockette who danced in the chorus line
came back to raise babies ten miles away.

The clamdigger brothers, working two tides a day,
sculpted like statues, left town in their prime.
The doctor brother returned to build homes,
the recovering teacher now fishes the sea.

The stenos, hairdressers, building inspectors
now all snuggle into the arms of the village.
People who married, those who traveled abroad
nestle into the homesteads built by their fathers.

Some born in the town migrate south in the winter,
reappear with songbirds early in spring.
The city-based clerk breathes deep of Maine air
as she crosses the Kittery bridge heading North.

Up on the hill among all the gravestones
lie the man shot dead in a place far from home
and a faraway baby who lived only a day.
Aunt Emma says, as she picks up a stitch,

"Our folks, they all come back in the end."

The Clerks

Edwin Arlington Robinson

I did not think that I should find them there
When I came back again; but there they stood,
As in the days they dreamed of when young blood
Was in their cheeks and women called them fair.
Be sure, they met me with an ancient air, —
And yes, there was a shop-worn brotherhood
About them; but the men were just as good,
And just as human as they ever were.

And you that ache so much to be sublime,
And you that feed yourself with your descent,
What comes of all your visions and your fears?
Poets and kings are but the clerks of Time,
Tiering the same dull webs of discontent,
Clipping the same sad alnage of the years.

Frenchboro

Susan Deborah King

Maybe on an outer island they don't care
as much how things look. Almost nothing
but lobster boats in this narrow harbor
their two-ways blaring into air otherwise pristine.
Very few pleasure craft.
Right by the dock, a wooden hull
collapsed, and is flattening,
boards slowly falling away from each other
like a body flummoxed by exhaustion.
The shed next to it, barely
holding together, windows
punched out, slumps.
Both just left, not cleaned up, built back,
hidden, cleared away or taken apart
and used for kindling.
Weather has made every effort to polish them.
Still, they're duller than tarnished silver.
They've given out, no good anymore,
not even for tuning the wind.
No one here pretends they are
or even gives a hoot.
Why do I find them beautiful?

Washington County, Maine

Tom Sexton

Apple trees heavy with the season's fruit,
piebald, yellow, planet-red, even black,
stand abandoned in fields, the unintended
gift of those who long ago moved on,
a gift to waxwings and even to the tone-
deaf crows in their undertaker's suits,
to the man driving slowly, window down,
to the worms in their snow-white orbit.

By Passamaquoddy Bay

Tom Sexton

Thin light over Campobello Island
to the east when I rise to walk
the long abandoned railroad bed.
Not a trace is left of the rails.
I have several letters to answer
and yesterday's paper to read,
but the wild apples are waiting
cold on the tongue, polished by mist.

Coming Home

Elizabeth Tibbetts

Oh, God, the full-faced moon is smiling at me
in his pink sky, and I'm alive, alive(!)
and driving home to you and our new refrigerator.
A skin of snow shines on the mountain beyond Burger King
and this garden of wires and poles and lighted signs.
Oh, I want to be new, I want to be the girl I saw
last night at the mike, sex leaking from her fingertips
as they traveled down to pick at her hem.
She was younger than I've ever been, with hair cropped,
ragged clothes, and face as clear as a child's.
She read as though she were in bed, eyes half closed,
teeth glistening, her shimmering body written
beneath her dress. She held every man in the audience
taut, and I thought of you. Now I'm coming home
dressed in my sensible coat and shoes, my purse
and a bundle of groceries beside me. When I arrive
we'll open the door of our Frigidaire
to its shining white interior, fill the butter's
little box, set eggs in their hollows, slip meats
and greens into separate drawers, and pause
in the newness of the refrigerator's light
while beside us, through the window,
the moon will lay a sheet on the kitchen floor.

Contributors

Richard Aldridge authored five volumes of poetry, including Driving North and Red Pine, Black Ash. He also edited three anthologies of poetry, the most recent of which was Speaking of New England. He was a secondary school teacher for several years and lived on the Maine coast.

Lynn Ascrizzi is an artist, poet, and freelance writer who lives with her husband Joe in a house they built in the woods of Freedom. Her poems have been published in *World Order*, *Xanadu*, *Orison VII*, and *Puckerbrush Review*. She was awarded the 1999 Robert Hayden Poetry Fellowship.

Carol Willette Bachofner is the Poet Laureate of Rockland. Her poems have appeared in *Prairie Schooner*, *The Cream City Review*, *The Comstock Review*, *Crab Orchard Review*, and *The Connecticut Review*. She has published three volumes of poetry. Her forthcoming collection is titled *Native Moons, Native Days*.

Former Maine poet laureate **Kate Barnes** is the daughter of Maine writers Henry Beston and Elizabeth Coatsworth. Her two collections of poetry are *Where the Deer Were* and *Kneeling Orion*. She has four grown children and resides on a farm in Appleton, which harvests blueberries and hay.

Louise Bogan was one of America's most important lyric poets. Her grandfather was a sea captain from Portland and she was born in Livermore Falls and returned to the state often, featuring its landscape in her poems and speaking, according to biographer Elizabeth Frank, with "a touch of Maine" in her voice.

Ted Bookey of Readfield is the author of five books of poems, most recently *With a W/hole in One*. He has also published, with his wife Ruth, a book of translations of the German poet Erich Kastner. Ted is the editor of the poetry anthology *How Many Cars Have We Been Married?*

The late **Philip Booth,** a resident of Castine, authored ten books of poetry and was often honored in his lifetime, continuing to be widely read. His prizes included awards from the Academy of American poets, the Rockefeller Foundation, the Guggenheim Foundation, and the National Institute of Arts and Letters.

Henry Braun is a retired professor from Temple University and a contributing editor for the *American Poetry Review.* His most recent book is *Loyalty: New and Selected Poems.* He lives with his wife Joan in Weld.

Sharon Bray of Orland farms family land on the tidal Penobscot River. Her work as a science writer, newspaper journalist, and poet has appeared in various forums, from medical and literary magazines to poetry anthologies.

Bob Brooks has published four chapbooks, most recently *Three-season Views* and *Companion Pieces.* His full-length collection *Unguarded Crossing* was recently named First Runner-up for the Eric Hoffer Book Award and shortlisted for the Maine Literary Award for poetry. He resides with his wife in Stockton Springs.

Linda Buckmaster has lived within a block of the Atlantic most of her life, growing up in "Space Coast" Florida and living for more than three decades in midcoast Maine. Former Poet Laureate of Belfast, she has published three chapbooks of poetry. Her poems, stories, and essays have been widely published.

Thomas Carper has authored three collections of formal poetry: *Fiddle Lane, From Nature,* and *Distant Blue.* He is coauthor with Derek Attridge of *Meter and Meaning: An Introduction to Rhythm in Poetry.* Professor Emeritus of English at the University of Southern Maine, he lives with his wife Janet in Cornish.

Robert M. Chute has published several collections of poetry, though his most recent books are the mysteries *Coming Home* and *Return to Sender.* He has received poetry prizes from the Maine Arts Commission and *The Beloit Poetry Review.* He lives in Poland Spring.

Elizabeth Coatsworth lived for many years with her husband, the writer Henry Beston, on a farm in Nobleboro. A versatile author, she published novels, nonfiction, and dozens of children's books, one of which received the Newbery Medal. She also wrote five collections of poetry.

Robert P. Tristram Coffin was a descendent of the original English settlers of Maine and an acclaimed historian of his time. He was also an essayist and poet, receiving the Pulitzer Prize for poetry in 1935. He attended Bowdoin and later taught there while writing many of his thirty-seven books.

Donald Crane lives on the Down East coast above Milbridge. Since retirement he has been able to pursue a life-long interest in poetry and has had poems published in a number of journals, including *The Café Review, The Christian Science Monitor, Passager,* and *Poetry East.*

Jay Davis lives in Portland, where he founded and hosted the Free Street Poetry Slam and The Skinny Second Tuesday Slam. His work has been published in *The Cafe Review, Monkey's Fist*, and other magazines. He has three chapbooks: *Whispers, Cries, and Tantrums*; *The Hard Way*; and *Socks.*

The late **Theodore Enslin's** early poetry was inspired by Temple, and after he moved to Milbridge in mid-life, he often wrote about the sea. He published numerous books of poetry, notably *Then and Now: New & Selected Poems*. Much of his later work was grounded in musical procedure.

Annie Farnsworth is an artist, Reiki master, gardener, and a poet, who has published a chapbook of poetry, *Bodies of Water, Bodies of Light*, as well as a full-length collection, *Angel of the Heavenly Tailgate*. She lives in Arundel with her partner, two children, and an assortment of animals.

Marta Rijn Finch shares the presidency of the Maine Poetry Society with her poet-mother, Maggie. She divides her time between Vermont and her home on Moosehead Lake. Her books include her recent collection, *A Solitary Piper*, and *Complete Poems: A Bilingual Edition*, a translation of the poems of Pernette de Guillet.

Richard Foerster is the author of six poetry collections, most recently *Penetralia*, which received the 2011 Maine Literary Award for Poetry. He has also been honored with two National Endowment for the Arts Fellowships and an Amy Lowell Poetry Traveling Scholarship. He lives in Cape Neddick.

Elizabeth W. Garber of Belfast is the author of *Listening Inside the Dance* and *Pierced by the Seasons*. Garrison Keillor has read three of her poems on *The Writer's Almanac*. She has promoted poetry as the 2006 Belfast Poet Laureate and as an organizer of the Belfast Poetry Festival.

Gerald George of East Machias has published four books and many articles and poems. His one-act plays have been produced by Acorn Productions and WERU radio. He serves on the editorial board of *Off the Coast*, and in 2010 was named as poet laureate of the Maine Senior College Network.

Bruce Guernsey, formerly a Distinguished Professor at Eastern Illinois University, has published poems in numerous magazines, including *Poetry, The Atlantic,* and *The American Scholar*. Among his collections are *January Thaw*, *New England Primer,* and most recently, *From Rain*. From 2006 to 2010, he edited *The Spoon River Poetry Review*. He lives in Bethel.

Ruth F. Guillard was born in Philadelphia and has a BFA degree from the University of Pennsylvania. A resident of Boothbay, she is a musician and teaches the Transcendental Meditation technique. She began writing poetry later in life and has recently published *From Burnham Cove*, a collection of her poems.

Peter Harris is the author of *Blue Hallelujahs,* which won the Maine Writers & Publishers Alliance Chapbook competition. He has published in places such as *The Atlantic, Ploughshares, Prairie Schooner, Seventeen Hills,* and *Sewanee Review.* He is a Zen priest who lives in Waterville and teaches at Colby College.

Nancy A. Henry has lived in Maine for thirty years. An attorney by education, she is now an adjunct professor at several Maine colleges. The co-founder, with Alice Persons, of Moon Pie Press, Nancy has published three full-length collections: *Sarx, Our Lady of Let's All Sing,* and *Who You Are.*

Preston H. Hood served in Vietnam with Seal Team 2 and was for fifteen years a member of Veterans for Peace. He has published two volumes of poetry: *A Chill I Understand* and the chapbook, *The Hallelujah of Listening,* which won the Maine Literary Award for Poetry. He lives in Sanford.

Sheila Gray Jordan lives year-round on Chebeague Island. She earned an MFA from the Warren Wilson Program for Writers. At Kenyon College she was an editor for *The Kenyon Review* and directed the Ohio Poetry Circuit. She has published two books of poetry: *Winter Wall* and *The China in the Sea.*

Stuart Kestenbaum is the author of three collections of poems, *Pilgrimage, House of Thanksgiving,* and *Prayers and Run-on Sentences,* as well as a book of essays on craft and community, *The View from Here.* He lives in Deer Isle, Maine, where he is the director of the Haystack Mountain School of Crafts.

Susan Deborah King has published four full-length collections of poems, two about the island in Maine where she lives with her family in the summer: *Bog Orchids* and *Tabernacle: Poems of an Island.* In winter, she teaches and writes in Minneapolis.

Gary Lawless is a Maine native who lives in Nobleboro. He is co-owner of Gulf of Maine Books, publisher of Blackberry Books, and a widely published poet, with seventeen collections published in the U.S. and four in Italy. He has read his poems in Italy, Slovenia, Latvia, Lithuania, Germany, and Cuba.

Carl Little started writing poetry as an undergraduate and won the Academy of American Poets Prize. His poems have appeared in many journals as well as in *Ocean Drinker: New & Selected Poems* and two anthologies of Maine poetry. He lives in Bar Harbor.

Kristen Lindquist lives and works in Camden. She received her MFA from the University of Oregon, and worked many years at the Bread Loaf Writers Conference. She has published two chapbooks, *Invocation to the Birds*, and most recently, *Transportation*. Her column, "The Natural World," appears monthly in the *Herald Gazette*.

Carolyn Locke, a resident of Troy, has done readings in various venues, including WERU radio and the Belfast Poetry Festival, and her work has twice been recognized by the Maine Literary Awards for Poetry.

Henry Wadsworth Longfellow was born in Portland and taught classics at Bowdoin College before joining the faculty at Harvard. A literary celebrity in his day, his narratives such as "The Song of Hiawatha" and "The Courtship of Miles Standish," provided a mythology for a developing America.

The late **Michael Macklin** lived in Portland and Islesboro. He served as a poetry editor for the *Cafe Review*, and on the board of The Maine Writers and Publishers Allliance, publishing his own poems in *Rattle, The Aurorean, Handsome*, and several anthologies. His chapbook of poems is titled *Driftland*.

Bob MacLaughlin lives in Warren. He has been a newspaper sportswriter, magazine editor, on-air promo writer for network TV, and an advertising copywriter doing print and broadcast. His book *Faulty Wiring: The Alzheimer's Poems and Other Memories* was published in 2011 by Moon Pie Press.

Mekeel McBride resides in Kittery, near the Piscataqua River. The author of several collections of poetry, she has received grants from the National Endowment for the Arts and a fellowship from the Bunting Institute. She volunteers at the Center for Wildlife in Cape Neddick, where she assists in rehabilitating wildlife.

The late **Elizabeth McFarland** served as poetry editor for *The Ladies Home Journal* from 1948 to 1961, providing six million readers for the work of the eminent American poets of her day. Her own poems, collected in *Over the Summer Water*, appeared posthumously in 2008, edited by her husband, the poet Daniel Hoffman.

Robin Merrill is a freelance writer and editor from Madison. Her poetry has appeared in numerous publications and has been featured on Garrison Keillor's *Writer's Almanac*. Her two volumes of poetry are *A House of Bottles* and *Laundry and Stories*. She has also written four children's books.

Edna St. Vincent Millay was born in Rockland and raised in Camden, and though she lived in New York City and settled in the Berkshires, she returned to Maine often, featuring it in her poems. Under eclipse for many years, her verse has been experiencing a much-deserved restoration.

Thomas R. Moore lives in Brooksville. His collection *The Bolt-Cutters* won the poetry prize in the Maine Literary Awards in 2011. Two of his poems have been featured on *The Writer's Almanac*. Two others were Pushcart Prize nominees, and one received a Pushcart Prize Special Mention.

David Moreau lives in Wayne with his wife and daughter. He has published four books of poetry. Two of his poems have been selected by Garrison Keillor for *The*

Writer's Almanac. David has worked supporting people with developmental disabilities for most of his adult life.

Dave Morrison's poetry has been published in both literary magazines and anthologies. *The Writers Almanac* featured two poems from his book *Clubland*, containing poems written in verse about rock bars. His eighth and most recent collection is titled *fail*. He lives in Camden.

Edward Nobles lives in Bangor with his wife Kelly, a Hermon High School English teacher. His poems have been published by numerous magazines, including the *Paris Review*, *Kenyon Review*, *Gettysburg Review,* and in *The Maine Poets* anthology. *Library Journal* selected Nobles as one of "24 Poets for the 21st Century."

Alice Persons of Westbrook has three poetry chapbooks and a full-length collection, *Thank Your Lucky Stars*. Eight of her poems have been read on Garrison Keillor's *Writer's Almanac*. She is the publisher of Moon Pie Press, which has listed sixty-one books of poetry since its inception in 2003.

Patricia Smith Ranzoni, a resident of Bucksport, has eight collections of poetry to her credit, most recently, Bedding Vows: Love Poems of Outback Maine. She has also published a workbook for children. Her work is being acquired by the Archives of Maine Writing and History.

Edward J. Rielly of Westbrook is a professor of English at Saint Joseph's College. He is the author or editor of approximately two dozen books, including twelve of poetry. Recent publications include *Legends of American Indian Resistance* and *To Sadie at 18 Months and Other Poems*.

Edwin Arlington Robinson lived much of his life before age thirty in Gardiner, the "Tilbury Town" of his poems. Provided by President Roosevelt with a clerkship that helped support him, he became a bestselling writer and won the Pulitzer Prize three times for poetry.

Kenneth Rosen lives in Portland. Among his titles are *The Origins of Tragedy, The Hebrew Lion, Reptile Mind,* and *No Snake, No Paradise.* His latest collection is *The Soul, O Ganders, Being Lonely, Flies.* His many poems in literary magazines are mainly uncollected.

Marija Sanderling is a librarian who has practiced creative writing since moving to Wells in 1994. Her poems, often concerned with social history and justice, have been published in *Cafe Review* and *Main Street Review.* Sanderling is a member of the Maine Poets Society.

A prolific writer of poetry, fiction, and nonfiction, **May Sarton** moved to York in the later part of her career, when she was rediscovered by feminist academics and reviewers, who found themes important to women in both her poetry and her nonfiction and hailed her as an important contemporary American author.

Tom Sexton is a former Poet Laureate of Alaska, an early editor of *Alaska Quarterly Review,* and founder of the creative writing program at the University of Alaska at Anchorage. Since 2001 he has lived part of the year in Eastport. His latest book is *I Think Again of Those Ancient Chinese Poets.*

Betsy Sholl, who lives in Portland, is the author of seven books of poetry, most recently *Rough Cradle.* She teaches at the University of Southern Maine and Vermont College of Fine Arts. She was Poet Laureate of Maine from 2006 to 2011.

The late **Robert Siegel** of South Berwick is the author of nine books of poetry and fiction, including *A Pentecost of Finches: New & Selected Poems* and *The Waters Under the Earth,* and received awards from *Poetry,* the Ingram Merrill Foundation, and the National Endowment for the Arts.

Pam Burr Smith lives in Brunswick. In 1995 she was awarded an Honorable Mention by Mary Oliver in the Maine Chapbook Contest. She has published poetry in many

Maine journals, including *Black Fly Review, Cafe Review, Animus,* and *Kennebec.* Her first book of poetry, *Heaven Jumping Woman,* was published in 2011.

Bruce Spang, Poet Laureate of Portland, teaches English at Scarborough High School. The editor of a recent anthology, *Passion and Pride: Poets In Support of Equality*, and author of two poetry collections, he lives in Falmouth. He is working on a new book, *Putting the Art Back in Language Arts.*

Martin Steingesser is the former Poet Laureate of Portland. His poems have also been published in *The Sun, The New York Times,* and *The American Poetry Review*, among other forums, as well as in his collection *Brothers of Morning.* He has performed his recent cycle of poems, *The Thinking Heart,* throughout Maine.

The late **John Tagliabue**'s first four volumes of poetry — *Poems, A Japanese Journal, The Buddha Uproar,* and *The Doorless Door* — preceded two later collections ranging over many years: *The Great Day: Poems, 1962–1983,* and *New and Selected Poems: 1942–1997*. Tagliabue taught poetry and literature at Bates and other schools around the world.

Ellen M. Taylor's work has appeared in literary journals throughout the United States. She has published two chapbooks of poetry and the full-length collection, *Floating*. Taylor teaches literature and Women's Studies at the University of Maine at Augusta and lives with her husband in Appleton.

Jim Glenn Thatcher lives in Yarmouth and teaches at Southern Maine Community College. He has an MFA from Vermont College and his poetry has won a number of honors, including five consecutive awards over the last two years from *New Millennium Writings*. He also published the chapbook, *The Ur-Word.*

Elizabeth Tibbetts's book of poems, *In the Well*, won the Bluestem Poetry Award. She has received a Maine Arts Commission Fellowship and a MAC Good Idea Grant, and her work has been featured on *The Writer's Almanac*. She lives with her husband in Hope and works as a nurse.

Mariana S. Tupper's poetry has appeared in *The Christian Science Monitor, Off the Coast, The Maine Times,* and *The Maine Organic Farmer & Gardener* newspaper. After many years of writing fiction and nonfiction, she "converted" to poetry at the turn of the century. She resides in Yarmouth.

Lewis Turco lives in Dresden Mills and is author of fifty-two books, including *The Book of Forms: A Handbook of Poetics,* called "the poets' Bible" since 1968. He has received many awards for his work, including honorary doctorates from The University of Maine at Fort Kent, Ashland University, and Unity College in Maine.

George V. Van Deventer, of Bristol, has served as Executive Director of the Live Poets Society and as editor of *Off the Coast.* In 1997 he developed poetry workshops in elementary schools, reaching more than a thousand students.

The late **David Walker**'s collection of poetry *Moving Out* won the poetry award in the Associated Writing Programs competition. His poetry was published in a number of national magazines and in three other collections, including *Voice Prints.*

Sarah Woolf-Wade, a retired teacher and a veteran sailor, lives in New Harbor. She has studied with poets John Holmes, Judith Steinbergh, Sam Hammill, and Billy Collins, among others. Her poems have appeared in many journals, newspapers, and anthologies; and in three collections of poetry, including *Nightsong.*

A former Ruth Lilly poet, **Douglas Woody Woodsum,** from Smithfield, has won an Avery Hopwood Award and the Bread Loaf Poetry Prize. He recently published the volume *The Lawns of Lobstermen.*

Index of Poets and Titles

Acknowledgments

Richard Aldridge: "Moth at My Window" copyright © 1980 by Richard Aldridge. Reprinted from *Red Pine, Black Ash,* Thorndike Press, 1980, by permission of the Estate of Richard Aldridge. "The Red and Green Cement Truck" copyright © 2001 by Richard Aldridge. Reprinted from *The Poems of Richard Aldridge,* 2001, by permission of Josephine Haskell Aldridge.

Lynn Ascrizzi: "New England Asters" copyright © 2012 by Lynn Ascrizzi. Reprinted from *Puckerbrush Review,* Puckerbrush Press Inc., 2012, by permission of Sandy Phippen.

Carol Willette Bachofner: "Loon Return" copyright © 2011 by Carol Willette Bachofner. Reprinted from *I Write in the Greenhouse,* Front Porch Books, 2011, by permission of Carol Willette Bachofner. "Unknown Algonquin Females" copyright © 2009 by Carol Willette Bachofner. Reprinted from *Crab Orchard Review,* 2009, by permission of Carol Willette Bachofner.

Kate Barnes: "Peaches" and "April and Then May" copyright © 1994 by David R. Godine. Reprinted from *Where the Deer Were,* David R. Godine, 1994, by permission of David R. Godine.

Louise Bogan: "Night," "Musician," "Question in a Field," and "To an Artist, To Take Heart" copyright © 1968 by Louise Bogan. Reprinted from *The Blue Estuaries: Poems: 1923–1968,* Farrar Straus and Giroux, New York, 1968, by permission of Farrar, Straus and Giroux.

Ted Bookey: "The Power of It" copyright © 2005 by Ted Bookey. Reprinted from *A Moxie and a Moon Pie: The Best of Moon Pie Press,* Volume 1, Moon Pie Press, 2005, by permission of Ted Bookey.

Philip Booth: "Old" and "United States" copyright © 1990 by Philip Booth. Reprinted from *Selves,* Penguin Publishing, 1990, by permission of Viking Penguin, a division of Penguin Group (USA) Inc. "Sixty" copyright © 1999 by Philip Booth. Reprinted from *Lifelines,* Penguin Publishing, 1999, by permission of Viking Penguin, a division of Penguin Group (USA) Inc.

Henry Braun: "Growing Lettuce" copyright © 2006 by Henry Braun. Reprinted from *Loyalty: New and Selected Poems,* Off the Grid Press, 2006, by permission of Henry Braun.

Sharon Bray: "1940" copyright © 2008 by Sharon Bray. Reprinted from *A Rump-Sprung Chair and a One-Eyed Cat,* Black Dog Press, 2008, by permission of Sharon Bray, Gerald George, and the Salt Coast Sages.

Bob Brooks: "Regret" and "Snap" copyright © 2011 by Bob Brooks. Reprinted from *Unguarded Crossing,* Antrim House, 2011, by permission of Bob Brooks.

Linda Buckmaster: "Sudden Death" and "January" copyright © 2007 by Linda Buckmaster. Reprinted from *Heart Song & Other Legacies,* Illuminated Sea Press, 2007, by permission of Linda Buckmaster.

Thomas Carper: "Roses" and "Nobody at Treblinka" copyright © 1991 by Thomas Carper. Reprinted from *Fiddle Lane,* John Hopkins University Press, 1991, by permission of Thomas Carper.

Robert M. Chute: "Driving Down East" copyright © 2010 by Robert M. Chute. Reprinted from *Maine Taproot,* Encircle Publications, 2010, by permission of Robert M. Chute.

Elizabeth Coatsworth: Poem copyright © 1968 by Elizabeth Coatsworth. Reprinted from *Down Half the World,* Macmillan, 1968, by permission of Kate Barnes.

Robert P. Tristram Coffin "Winter Friends" copyright © 1948 by Robert P. Tristram Coffin. Reprinted from *Collected Poems of Robert P. Tristram Coffin,* The Macmillan Company, American Book - Stratford Press, 1948, by permission of the estate of Robert P. Tristram Coffin.

Donald Crane: "Divorce" copyright © 2008 by Donald Crane. Reprinted from *Puckerbrush Review,* Winter/Spring 2008, Puckerbrush Press, 2008, by permission of Donald Crane.

Jay Davis: "Potatoes" copyright © 2004 by Jay Davis. Reprinted from *Whispers, Cries, and Tantrums,* Moon Pie Press, 2004, by permission of Jay Davis.

Theodore Enslin: "The Glass Harmonica" copyright © 1958 by Theodore Enslin. Reprinted from *Then and Now,* National Poetry Foundation Press, 1999, by permission of Theodore Enslin.

Annie Farnsworth: "Spaghetti Western Days" copyright © 2006 by Annie Farnsworth. Reprinted from *Angel of the Heavenly Tailgate,* Moon Pie Press, 2006, by permission of Annie Farnsworth. "For the Falling Man" copyright © 2001 by Annie Farnsworth. Reprinted from *Bodies of Water, Bodies of Light,* Sheltering Pine Press, 2001, by permission of Annie Farnsworth.

Marta Rijn Finch: "The Poet" copyright © 2011 by Marta Rijn Finch. Reprinted from *A Solitary Piper,* Encircle Publications, 2011, by permission of Marta Rijn Finch.

Richard Foerster: "Garden Spider" copyright © 2002 by Richard Foerster. Reprinted from *Double Going,* BOA Editions, Ltd., 2005, by permission of Richard Foerster. "Fiddleheads" copyright © 1998 by Richard Foerster. Reprinted from *Trillium,* BOA Editions, Ltd., 1998, by permission of Richard Foerster.

Elizabeth W. Garber: "Feasting" copyright © 2004 by Elizabeth W. Garber. Reprinted from *Pierced by the Seasons,* The Illuminated Sea Press, 2004, by permission of Elizabeth W. Garber.

Gerald George: "Rained Out" copyright © 2008 by Gerald George. Reprinted from *A Rump-Sprung Chair and a One-Eyed Cat,* Black Dog Press, 2008, by permission of Gerald George, Sharon Bray, and the Salt Coast Sages.

Bruce Guernsey: "The Dump Pickers" copyright © 2012 by Bruce Guernsey. Reprinted from *From Rain: Poems 1970–2010,* Ecco Qua Press, 2012, by permission of Bruce Guernsey. "Night Patrol" and "The Hands" copyright © 2004 by Water Press & Media. Reprinted from *The Lost Brigade,* Water Press & Media, 2004, by permission of Water Press & Media.

Ruth F. Guillard: "Spring Thaw" copyright © 2011 by Ruth F. Guillard: Reprinted from *Transitions,* Adagio Press, 2011, by permission of Ruth F. Guillard.

Peter Harris: "The Net" copyright © 1999 by Peter Harris. Reprinted from *The Atlantic Monthly,* 1999, by permission of Peter Harris.

Nancy A. Henry: "From the Toy Box" copyright © 2002 by Nancy A. Henry. Reprinted from *SARX,* Moon Pie Press, 2010, by permission of Nancy A. Henry.

Preston H. Hood: "Cullen: Four Days Old, Waking" copyright © 2011 by Preston H. Hood. Reprinted from *The Hallelujah of Listening,* Červená Barva Press, 2011, by permission of Preston H. Hood.

Sheila Gray Jordan: "The Man Who Likes Cows" copyright © 1995 by Sheila Gray Jordan. Reprinted from *The China in the Sea,* Signal Books, 1995, by permission of Sheila Gray Jordan. "In Nightgowns" copyright © 2010 by Sheila Gray Jordan. Reprinted from *Winter Wall,* Stone Sleep Books, 2010, by permission of Sheila Gray Jordan.

Stuart Kestenbaum: "Essence" copyright © 2003 by Stuart Kestenbaum. Reprinted from *House of Thanksgiving,* Deerbrook Editions, 2003, by permission of Stuart Kestenbaum. "Mr. Fix-It" and "April Prayer" copyright © 2007 by Stuart Kestenbaum.

Reprinted from *Prayers & Run-on Sentences,* Deerbrook Editions, 2007, by permission of Stuart Kestenbaum.

Susan Deborah King: "Watermelon" and "Frenchboro" copyright © 2010 by Susan Deborah King. Reprinted from *Bog Orchids,* The Island Institute, 2010, by permission of Susan Deborah King.

Gary Lawless: "Some Clear Night" and "Which World" copyright © 1998 by Gary Lawless. Reprinted from *Caribouddhism,* Blackberry Books, 1998, by permission of Gary Lawless.

Carl Little: "Zones of Peeper" copyright © 2009 by Carl Little. Reprinted from *Down East* magazine, March 2009, by permission of Carl Little. "Last Writes" copyright © 2010 by Carl Little. Reprinted from *Off the Coast,* Fall 2010, by permission of Carl Little.

Kristen Lindquist: "Transportation" copyright © 2001 by Kristen Lindquist. Reprinted from *Invocation to the Birds,* Oyster River Press, 2001, by permission of Kristen Lindquist.

Carolyn Locke: "Regeneration" copyright © 2010 by Carolyn Locke. Reprinted from *Always this Falling,* Maine Authors Publishing, 2010, by permission of Carolyn Locke.

Michael Macklin: "Resurrection" copyright © 2004 by Michael Macklin. Reprinted from *A Moxie and A Moon Pie: The Best of Moon Pie Press*, Moon Pie Press, 2005, by permission of Michael Macklin.

Bob MacLaughlin: "Ball Smacks Mouth, Splits Lip" copyright © 2011 by Bob MacLaughlin. Reprinted from *Faulty Wiring: the Alzheimer's Poems and Other Memories,* Moon Pie Press, 2001, by permission of Bob MacLaughlin.

Mekeel McBride: "The Goldfish" and "Where Inspiration Has Learned a Thing or Two" copyright © 2006 by Mekeel McBride. Reprinted from *Dog Star Delicatessen,* Carnegie Mellon University Press, 2006, by permission of Mekeel McBride. "A Little Bit of Timely Advice" copyright © 1995 by Mekeel McBride. Reprinted from *Wind of the White Dresses,* Carnegie Mellon University Press, 1995, by permission of Mekeel McBride.

Elizabeth McFarland: "Feed My Birds" copyright © 1984 by Elizabeth McFarland. Reprinted from *Over the Summer Water,* Orchises Press, 2008, by permission of Daniel G. Hoffman, Trustee, Estate of Elizabeth McFarland Hoffman.

Robin Merrill: "Out Here" copyright © 2005 by Robin Merrill. Reprinted from *Laundry and Stories,* Moon Pie Press, 2005, by permission of Robin Merrill.

Edna St. Vincent Millay: "Love Is Not All: It Is Not Meat Nor Drink," "To Jesus on His Birthday," and "Hearing Your Words, and Not a Word Among Them" copyright © 1931, 1958 by Edna St. Vincent Millay and Norma Millay Ellis. Reprinted by permission of Holly Peppe, Literary Executor, The Millay Society.

Thomas R. Moore: "Her Telling" and "The Plymouth on Ice" copyright © 2010 by Thomas R. Moore. Reprinted from *The Bolt-Cutters,* Fort Hemlock Press, 2010, by permission of Thomas R. Moore.

David Moreau: "Salt to the Brain" copyright © 2005 by David Moreau. Reprinted from *A Movie and a Moon Pie: The Best of Moon Pie Press,* Volume 1, Moon Pie Press, 2005, by permission of David Moreau.

Dave Morrison: "Closing Time" and "He Sees the Future" copyright © 2011 by Dave Morrison. Reprinted from *Clubland*, Fighting Cock Press, 2011, by permission of Dave Morrison.

Edward Nobles: "Sentences" copyright © 2000 by Edward Nobles. Reprinted from *The Bluestone Walk*, Persea Books, 2000, by permission of Edward Nobles. "Where He Went" copyright © 2010 by Edward Nobles.

Alice Persons: "Mud Season" copyright © 2005 by Alice Persons. Reprinted from *A Moxie and a Moon Pie: The Best of Moon Pie Press*, Volume 1, Moon Pie Press, 2005, by permission of Alice Persons. "Stealing Lilacs" copyright © 2004 by Alice Persons. Reprinted from *Never Say Never*, Moon Pie Press, 2004, by permission of Alice Persons.

Patricia Smith Ranzoni: "Housekeeping of a Kind" copyright © 1995 by Patricia Ranzoni. Reprinted from *Claiming*, Puckerbrush Press, 1995, by permission of Patricia Ranzoni. "If You Should Die Before I Do" copyright © 2000 by Patricia Ranzoni. Reprinted from *Settling*, Puckerbrush Press, 2000, by permission of Patricia Ranzoni.

Edward J. Rielly: "Hands Reaching" copyright © 2005 by Edward J. Rielly. Reprinted from *Ways of Looking: Poems of the Farm*, Moon Pie Press, 2005, by permission of Edward J. Rielly.

Kenneth Rosen: "The Last Lamplighters" and "The Alligator's Hum" copyright © 2003 by Kenneth Rosen. Reprinted from *The Origins of Tragedy & Other Poems*, CavanKerry Press, 2003, by permission of Kenneth Rosen.

Marija Sanderling: "Free Agent" copyright © 2010 by Marija Sanderling. Reprinted from *Maine Taproot*, Encircle Publications, 2010, by permission of Marija Sanderling.

May Sarton: "Death and the Turtle," "A Parrot," and "The Geese" copyright © 1993, 1988, 1984, 1980, 1974 by May Sarton. Reprinted from *Collected Poems: 1930-1993*, W. W. Norton & Company, Inc., by permission of W. W. Norton & Company, Inc.

Tom Sexton: "Porcupine" copyright © 2009 by Tom Sexton. Reprinted from *For the Sake of the Light,* University of Alaska Press, 2009, by permission of Tom Sexton. "Washington County, Maine" and "By Passamaquoddy Bay" copyright © 2011 by Tom Sexton. Reprinted from *I Think Again of Those Ancient Chinese Poets,* University of Alaska Press, 2011, by permission of Tom Sexton.

Betsy Sholl: "Gulls in Wind" copyright © 2003 by Betsy Sholl. Reprinted from *The Maine Times,* 2003, by permission of Betsy Sholl. "To the Infinitesimal" copyright © 2009 by Betsy Sholl. Reprinted from *Rough Cradle,* Alice James Books, 2009, by permission of Alice James Books, Farmington, Maine.

Robert Siegel: "How to Catch a Poem," "Mantis," "Nude," and "Airfield" copyright © 2001 by Robert Siegel. Reprinted from *A Pentecost of Finches: New and Selected Poems,* Paraclete Press, 2006, by permission of Robert Siegel.

Pam Burr Smith: "Sandwiches" copyright © 2011 by Pam Burr Smith. Reprinted from *Heaven Jumping Woman,* Moon Pie Press, 2011, by permission of Pam Burr Smith.

Bruce Spang: "Humane Society" copyright © 2002 by Bruce Spang. Reprinted from *The Knot,* Snowdrift Press, 2002, by permission of Bruce Spang.

Martin Steingesser: "Today the Traffic Signals All Changed for Me" and "Mom Gets in One of My Poems" copyright © 2012 by Martin Steingesser. Reprinted from *Brothers of Morning,* Deerbrook Editions, 2012, by permission of Martin Steingesser.

John Tagliabue: "What Position Do They and We Assume in the Encapsulated Stillness?" copyright © 1997 by John Tagliabue. Reprinted from *New and Selected Poems: 1942–1997,* National Poetry Foundation Press, 1997, by permission of the estate of John Tagliabue.

Ellen M. Taylor: "Spring Cleaning," "Hummingbird," and "Hen" copyright © 2009 by Ellen M. Taylor. Reprinted from *Floating,* Moon Pie Press, 2009, by permission of Ellen M. Taylor.

Jim Glenn Thatcher: "Understory" copyright © 2008 by Jim Glenn Thatcher. Reprinted from *The Ur-Word*, Moon Pie Press, 2008, by permission of Jim Glenn Thatcher.

Elizabeth Tibbetts: "Eighty-five" and "Coming Home" copyright © 2002 by Elizabeth Tibbetts. Reprinted from *In the Well,* Bluestem Press at Emporia State University, 2002, by permission of Elizabeth Tibbetts.

Mariana S. Tupper: "My Hairy Legs" copyright © 2006 by Mariana S. Tupper. Reprinted from *Off the Coast*, May 2006, Resolute Bear Press, by permission of Mariana S. Tupper.

Lewis Turco: "The Street" and "The Habitation" copyright © 2007 by Lewis Turco. Reprinted from *Fearful Pleasures: The Complete Poems of Lewis Turco 1959–2007,* Star Cloud Press, 2007, by permission of Lewis Turco.

George V. Van Deventer: "Early Morning Trumpet" copyright © 1988 by George V. Van Deventer. Printed by permission George V. Van Deventer.

David Walker: "The Crossing" copyright © 1976 by the Rector and Visitors of the University of Virginia. Reprinted from "Moving Out," University Press of Virginia, 1976, by permission of Rector and Visitors of the University of Virginia.

Sarah Woolf-Wade: "Making the Turn" and "They All Come Back" copyright © 2008 by Sarah Jane Woolf-Wade. Reprinted from *Down the Bristol Road*, Snow Drift Press, 2008, by permission of Sarah Jane Woolf-Wade.

Douglas Woody Woodsum: "Spooked Moose" copyright © 2007 by Douglas Woodsum. Reprinted from *Down East,* Down East Enterprise, Inc., October 2007, by permission of Douglas Woodsum.

Called by poet Philip Levine one of the great storytellers of contemporary poetry, **Wesley McNair** is the author of twenty books, including his current titles, *Lovers of the Lost: New and Selected Poems* and *The Words I Chose: A Memoir of Family and Poetry*. He has twice been invited by the Library of Congress to read his poetry, and has won the Robert Frost and Theodore Roethke Prizes, grants from the Fulbright and Guggenheim Foundations, two Rockefeller Fellowships, and two grants in poetry from the National Endowment for the Arts. In 2006 he was selected for a United States Artist Fellowship as one of America's finest living artists. He is Maine's Poet Laureate.